PENNSYLVANIA COUNTRY ANTIQUES

PENNSYLVANIA COUNTRY ANTIQUES

Albert T. Gamon

PRENTICE-HALL, INC.
ENGLEWOOD CLIFFS, NEW JERSEY

Dedicated to Charles Supplee
Friend and Mentor

———————————

PENNSYLVANIA COUNTRY ANTIQUES

FOREWORD

Anyone who has gone to the trouble to choose this book from the shelf is already interested in its subject matter. We feel, however, that the writing of another book on antiques deserves an explanation of our purpose. A glance at a list of publications would show that numerous articles and books have been written about virtually every type of collectables, from matchboxes to steam locomotives, and that American furniture from Jamestown to Grand Rapids has been discussed, dissected, scoured, scraped, refinished, and restored down to the last detail. A longer look at the same list, however, would reveal that in all this wealth of information there is an amazing dearth of material on the furniture of rural Pennsylvania, excepting that of Pennsylvania German derivation. This lack becomes all the more regrettable when one realizes that Pennsylvania was one of the original colonies and a veritable melting pot of people from other lands. The shapes and styles of our early country furniture were influenced by the tastes and customs of the Swedes, the Swiss, the Welsh, the Irish, the Scottish, the French, and the English, as well as the Palatine Germans (Pennsylvania Dutch). Beyond this, of course, our country cabinetmakers and craftsmen undoubtedly felt the influence, albeit somewhat late, of the more sophisticated craftsmen working in the nearby furniture centers of Philadelphia, Baltimore, and New York.

Although furniture was handcrafted in Pennsylvania from the time of arrival of the first settlers in 1638, at what is now the city of Chester, until the end of the nineteenth century, it is not the purpose of this book to discuss objects that can be seen only in museums. It is instead to help acquaint the reader with some of the examples of antique furniture available today throughout the countryside. If you are looking for information on Queen Anne tables, Chippendale desks, or Philadelphia highboys, this book will not be of help. But if you are trying to furnish a solid old Pennsylvania farmhouse in a manner reflecting its simple charm, or if you wish to create a country feeling in a new split-level home, or if you simply are attracted by the look and the history of country furniture, this book will provide you with detailed descriptions of the type of furniture which will suit your taste.

Most of the pieces which will be discussed were made during, or have the flavor of, the years 1750 to 1860. No furniture made after 1890 will be discussed, since even in the hinterlands that date marked the end of handcrafted furniture. The qualifying phrase "or have the flavor of" has had to be inserted because of the difficulty of dating country-made furniture. "Style," often the basis for dating the formal furniture produced in the cities, is almost worthless in dating country furniture. It is not unheard-of to come across a dated piece still showing strong influence of one of the great cabinetmakers, but made fifty years *after* its style had lost popularity in the cities. (A piece such as this would be, in the parlance of the trade, a "survival" example.) Even construction details lose a great deal of relevance when we try to date furniture made by our country craftsmen. These men were traditionally slow to change, so that methods used by their fathers and grandfathers were continued long after more modern methods were introduced in the cities. Wooden pegs, for instance, were used to hold country tables together long after the city craftsmen had accepted glue; and slow, costly transportation from the cities kept local blacksmiths in business providing hand-wrought nails and hinges for nearby cabinetmakers many years after such hardware had become obsolete in urban areas. Consequently, the Latin word "circa" as used in this or any other book concerning country furniture must be interpreted a good deal more loosely than is customary in the study of more formal furniture. "Circa" here will mean "plus or minus about twenty years from the date mentioned," and we hope this will be reasonably accurate.

The reader will notice in our discussion the absence of the phrase "primitive furniture." The word "primitive" conjures up images of unskilled work and poor craftsmanship, which have nothing whatever to do with the beautiful dovetailing of a pine blanket chest, the rat-tail hinges of a cherry Dutch cupboard, or other details which characterize the furniture we will be discussing.

It should also be noted that many of the terms used throughout this book will be unfamiliar to some readers. To avoid confusion and to assure that the reader derives the same meaning as we from those more specialized words and phrases, we have included, directly after the text, a glossary of terms unique to the study of antiques.

We have heard it said many times that "antiques are where you find them," and we certainly have no quarrel with that statement. However, we can be somewhat systematic in our search for Pennsylvania country furniture. The great majority of the earlier pieces still available are to be found in the areas of the state which were settled first. Thus the counties which surround the cities of Philadelphia and Lancaster—Bucks, Montgomery, Chester, Lehigh, Berks,

Lancaster, Lebanon, and Dauphin—have long been fertile areas in which to search. Nor should the western areas be ignored. Many fine examples of furniture have come to light in such western counties as Fayette, Cambria, Westmoreland, Indiana, and Somerset, where the rivers of western Pennsylvania gave rise to a number of early settlements, among them Pittsburgh, founded by the French as Fort Duquesne in 1754. A glance at a map will show why some of the northern counties have not proven particularly bountiful for antique collectors. Many of these counties, which are sparsely settled today, were only wilderness when the furniture which we will discuss was being made.

Other than through inheritance, there are two methods by which country antiques can be acquired today. They either can be bought from a reputable dealer, or if one is endowed with great patience, at one of the many auctions that dot the countryside every Saturday. There are still occasional bargains to be found at country auctions ("sales" to the initiates), but they are scarce. Dealers themselves use the auctions to replenish their stock, and it is seldom that a "sleeper" gets by these canny individuals. If however, you have plenty of spare time, if you know how to look before you buy, and if you don't mind disappointment, then by all means give the "sales" a try. Notices of coming auctions are published in small town newspapers throughout the state, and they always include the location of the sale, usually with directions for getting there. Most of the sales are held during the warm months, and the majority are on Saturdays, but there are some areas of the state where one could go to a sale every day of the week, every week of the year, Sundays excepted of course.

It is no longer worthwhile for the average collector to drive through the countryside looking for bargains, since any attractive piece that he should happen to "find" has probably already been found by a dealer or a picker and a fair price offered for it. The fact that it is still in the possession of its owner indicates either that he believes it to be worth more than the price offered or that it is a family heirloom and not available at any price.

The least time-consuming and, in the long run, the cheapest way to find good antiques is to visit the shops of reputable dealers. Many of the counties listed above have associations of antique dealers, and all of these associations are glad to furnish a list of their members. During a visit to one of the annual or semi-annual shows sponsored by each of these groups, one can view at first hand a large variety of the antiques currently available and meet many of the dealers in that particular county. By and large, these dealers are men and women who can be trusted to represent their merchandise properly and charge no more than the going price. In addition to the time saved by buying from a dealer, the furniture bought is usually completely restored and ready for use. Furniture bought at auction is almost always "in the rough," and the purchaser might well find that by the time he has a usable piece, far more has been paid for it than would have been had he bought it from a dealer in the first place.

It seems to be the duty of every writer to close his foreword by extending thanks to all the people who assisted him in his efforts. In this case the duty is a decided pleasure. The somewhat trite phrase, "without whose help this book could not have been written," has never been more true. I am particularly grateful for the cooperation and interest shown by the staffs of The Philadelphia Museum of Art, The Pennsylvania Farm Museum of Landis Valley, The Mercer Museum of the Bucks County Historical Society, The Chester County Historical Society, and The Pennsylvania Historical Society. I would also like to express my sincere thanks to the many good people who have welcomed me into their homes and shops to photograph and take notes, to the dealers who have placed their knowledge and time at my disposal, and to my wife—without whose forbearance (and spelling aptitude) this book most certainly would not have been written.

ILLUSTRATIONS

LIST OF PHOTOGRAPHS

16

All photographs not otherwise noted are of articles from the author's collection.

LIST OF DRAWINGS

CONTENTS

PENNSYLVANIA COUNTRY ANTIQUES

CHAPTER ONE

TABLES AND STANDS

It would seem appropriate to begin a book of this nature with the article of furniture first needed and hence first produced by our early settlers. The newcomers to these shores usually arrived with only their household goods, their personal belongings, and a few tools packed in boxes and chests; the crowded conditions aboard ship prevented their bringing any other furniture with them. The settler's first requirement was, of course, housing. But it is safe to assume that as soon as a shelter was erected the womenfolk thought about furnishing it. The boxes and chests they had brought with them made reasonably good substitutes for chairs, and even occasionally for beds, but there never has been a housewife content for long without a table for the family to gather around at meals. Thus tables were probably among the first articles of furniture to be built during the settling of our eastern counties. Any of these very early tables that still exist, however, have long since gone into museums or private collections, so we will confine our attention to tables of later vintage.

In attempting to determine the age of a table, one can look for several specific indicators in addition to general signs of age (which will be discussed in Chapter 9). The method by which the top of the table was attached to the apron is an indicator applicable to all varieties of tables. The earliest method was to fasten the top by means of wooden pegs; later tops were secured by hand-forged nails, and still later ones by screws. The better examples were always toe-nailed (or screwed) from the bottom at an angle through the inside of the apron; cruder examples were nailed straight down through the top. Another method used extensively in Pennsylvania was to fasten the top to the rest of the table by means of large removable pins, which were inserted into the apron through battens secured to the underside of the top. Cleats or battens on the *ends* (not the bottoms) of tabletops generally indicate construction prior to 1750, and so predate the period covered by this book.

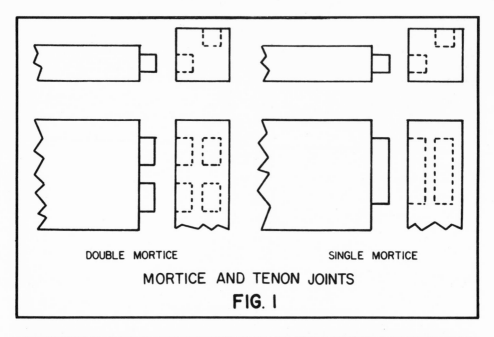

DOUBLE MORTICE   SINGLE MORTICE

MORTICE AND TENON JOINTS

FIG. I

1. Folding trestle table, Pine, Circa 1760

Courtesy of Mr. and Mrs. Charles Supplee   *Photograph by Charles R. Steitz, Jr.*

2. Sawbuck table, Pine, Circa 1800
Courtesy of Mr. David King   *Photograph by Charles R. Steitz, Jr.*

On early tables the legs were attached to the apron by double mortice and tenon joints, while on later ones single mortice and tenon joints were used (see Figure 1). We can only assume that the double joint was used in an effort to prevent the apron from splitting as the wood dried out and contracted (see the section on shrinkage, Chapter 9).

The earliest tables in Pennsylvania were probably of the trestle type, which general category includes the familiar sawbuck table. Genuine tables of this type are so early and so rare that we will do little except to call attention to them in Plates 1 and 2 and to warn that trestle tables, far from being unique to Pennsylvania, were made until the late nineteenth century in the Shaker communities of New York State and New England.

Another type of table which was made in some quantity in rural Pennsylvania, but which also predates the span covered by this book, is the large tavern (also called kitchen or stretcher) table (Plate 3). This style was made from about 1660 to about 1740, and the only reason to mention it here is to show its similarity to the farm table, its direct descendant.

3. Large tavern table in the Tavern Kitchen of The Pennsylvania Farm Museum of Landis Valley

Courtesy of the museum   *Photograph by Charles R. Steitz, Jr.*

Farm Tables

As indicated, the Pennsylvania farm table is a descendant of the large tavern table, differing from the earlier style chiefly in its lack of stretchers. The very name "farm table" is a rather recent innovation, and many dealers and col-

4. Large farm table, Walnut, Circa 1830
Courtesy of Mr. and Mrs. Robert Levison   *Photograph by Charles R. Steitz, Jr.*

lectors still mistakenly refer to tables of this type as tavern tables. They are found in many sizes, with tops ranging from 3 by 5 feet to 4 by 8 feet, with turned or square legs (straight or tapered), and with one to three drawers. We have arbitrarily chosen to classify them here by size according to their number of drawers; thus we have called those with two and three drawers "large," as in Plate 4, and those with only one drawer "small." The large ones are most often of walnut, pine, or cherry (in that order of frequency), while the small ones are usually of pine. The planks which form the top of a large farm table are held together by cleats on the underside, and the cleats in turn are fastened to the apron with large removable wooden pins, thus fastening the top to the rest of the table and still making it easily removable. The small ones usually do not have this arrangement. The larger farm tables no doubt were built to be used as eating tables in the kitchen, and they still serve admirably in this capacity. They may also be used to good advantage as dining room tables when the additional size of a drop leaf is not required. The smaller ones were probably used as work

5. Small farm table, Pine, Circa 1830   *Photograph by Charles R. Steitz, Jr.*

tables in the kitchen and can still be used as such. One of the small ones can also work quite nicely as a flat-topped desk, as does the one pictured in Plate 5.

Tavern Tables (Small)

These small tables were used in our early inns and taverns for serving the patrons who did not care to eat (or drink) at one of the common tables. The host would carry the small table to the patron and place it over his knees, thus permitting him to sit wherever he pleased. Since these tables were designed to be portable, they were invariably light in weight and consequently not very strong. The table pictured in Plate 6, with its pine top and apron and its poplar legs, weighs only 11 pounds. This light construction probably accounts for the relative scarcity of this type of table today—they simply were not capable of withstanding the kind of punishment they received in the day-to-day activities of our early taverns. When found today, they usually require extensive repairs, as was the case with the example in Plate 6, which had one leg secured by a sheet

6. Small tavern table, Pine, Circa 1835. The square tapered legs are a survival feature of the Hepplewhite period. *Photograph by Charles R. Steitz, Jr.*

of tin, the top of the leg having almost completely disintegrated. Obviously of country origin and made about 1835, this table has a decided Hepplewhite feeling in its slim, square, tapered legs, but since Hepplewhite went out of style in the cities after about 1810, this piece must be classified as a survival example.

There has been some disagreement over the original purpose of a piece of furniture such as this—whether it was designed as a table or a stand. The dividing line between the two is rather thin, but it seems to us that a table of this type is usually lighter, and its top usually larger, than would be appropriate to a stand. The piece shown has a top measuring 18 by 26½ inches, just about the right size for one table setting and a little elbow room. Its use is further indicated by its lack of a drawer, for which there would be no need, and its lack of stretchers or a low shelf, the presence of which would not allow it to be placed over a customer's knees. Finally, it is 30 inches high, just about the proper height for an eating table.

Gate-leg Tables

Gate-leg tables were introduced in the seventeenth century, and although Pennsylvania has no claim to their origin, their prevalence throughout the state is reason to include them here (Plate 7). Their popularity was due at least as much to their practicality as to their beauty. Closed, they occupy about one third the space they require when open, yet their full size is immediately available when needed—an asset just as valuable now as it was when they were new (see Plate 8).

These tables almost invariably have turned legs, usually of some form of vase turning, which on country examples is not often as well executed as on city-made tables. The examples encountered outside the cities are almost always of the six-leg (as opposed to the eight-leg) variety, with one gate leg supporting a leaf on each side of the table. Tables of the period with which we are concerned were made without the stretchers that were considered necessary in prior years.

The leaves were rectangular or semi-oval and often made of one wide board which reached almost to the floor when folded. On these tables the ends of the central section of the top always conformed to the shape of the leaves. If the table originally had curved leaves, when open it will present a complete oval or elliptical configuration, with the outer ends of the leaves flowing in a smooth curve into the ends of the top. Thus if a table is found with a top that has a rectangular central section but rounded leaves, the finder can be quite sure that the leaves have been altered. The treatment of the edge of the top of country pieces is usually plain, with no attempt at mold.

7. Gate-leg table, Cherry, Circa 1840

Courtesy of Mr. and Mrs. J. V. James   *Photograph by Bowen Studio*

The hinge connecting the gate leg to the rest of the table (see Figure 2) is usually of wood, with a metal pin. It is constructed so that the two members meet much like a box dovetail, and the stationary member is secured flat against the apron of the table. The apron of the gate section (which is also the leaf of the gate hinge) is usually of the same width and depth as the rest of the apron.

Walnut seems to have been the favorite wood for these tables, with cherry running a close second. Pine was also used for tops and aprons, in combination with maple or some other hardwood for the legs.

Many times a table will be found with the feet partially worn away, particularly the feet of the gate legs. This is normal wear and is the result of the movement of the feet across the floor as the leaves were raised and lowered.

33

8. Dining room in "The Cliffs" in Fairmount Park, Philadelphia, Pa. Notice the gate-leg table and rush-seated ladder-back chair.

Photograph courtesy of The Philadelphia Museum of Art

The earliest drop-leaf and gate-leg tables had either a plain butt joint (Figure 3A) or a groove joint (Figure 3B) where the leaf met the top. These were both replaced by the rule joint (Figure 3C) around 1825. This joint, when properly executed, allows no visible gap between the top and the leaves and consequently has been used almost exclusively since its inception. The butt joint is occasionally found on crude tables of a much later vintage, produced by unskilled workers, but furniture of this sort seldom has any antique value.

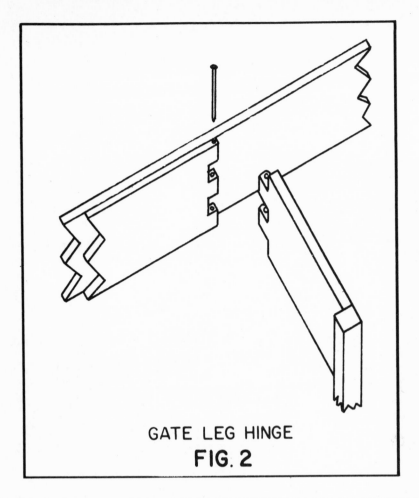

GATE LEG HINGE

FIG. 2

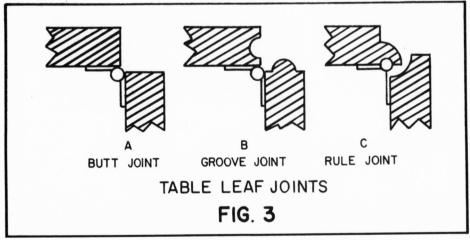

A
BUTT JOINT

B
GROOVE JOINT

C
RULE JOINT

TABLE LEAF JOINTS

FIG. 3

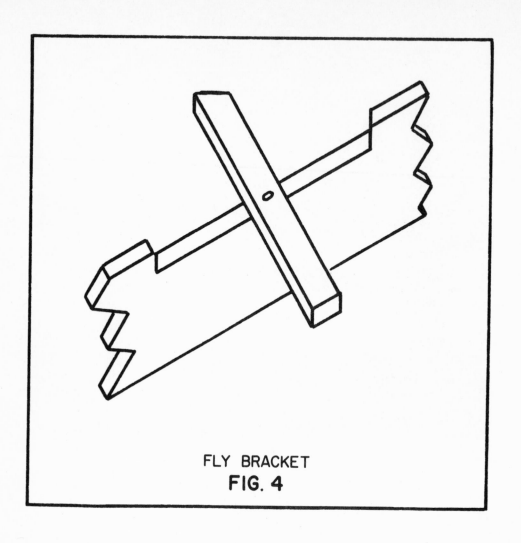

FLY BRACKET
FIG. 4

Drop-leaf Tables

Most of what has been said about the gate-leg table also applies to the drop-leaf table. The differences are that the leaves on the drop-leaf table are not as wide and that they are supported by a swinging arm (fly bracket), instead of by a gate leg (see Figure 4 and Plate 9). These tables were made to be used as kitchen tables or as occasional tables elsewhere in the home, and it is thought that those with a drawer were intended for use in the kitchen. Whatever their makers' intentions, most old drop-leaf tables have seen kitchen duty at one time or another, as is evidenced by the many layers of paint which usually adorn them. Taking the trouble to remove the paint is well worth the effort if the table's structure is in reasonably good condition, since its refinishing will result

9. Drop-leaf table, Cherry, Circa 1860   *Photograph by Charles R. Steitz, Jr.*

in a table of pleasing, if simple lines, strongly reminiscent of its more sophisticated cousin, the Pembroke.

Hutch Tables

Although hutch tables are by no means native to Pennsylvania and are not prevalent in this state, enough are found of Pennsylvania provenance to warrant their inclusion here. The name comes from the "hutch" or cubby often found below the top. It is a piece of furniture of considerable versatility, usable as a box for storage at the same time it is being used as a table or bench. The top of a hutch table is fastened by pins, through battens on its underside, to four uprights which also form the legs and feet of the table. Between these uprights there is often a box, so constructed that its hinged lid is just far enough above the floor to be used as a seat. Removal of two of the pins permits the top to be swung up upon the remaining two, thus converting the table into a bench with a large back formed by the now vertical top. Altogether a very practical piece of furni-

10. Hutch table, Pine, Circa 1820

Courtesy of Mr. and Mrs. Charles Supplee   *Photograph by Charles R. Steitz, Jr.*

ture, the hutch lends itself nicely to today's small kitchens. It even provides an ideal storage place for galoshes, overshoes, and other articles that never seem to have a place to hide. Hutch tables can be found with round, oval, square, or rectangular tops, ranging in size from tiny ones of about 2 feet square to huge ones of about 7 by 4 feet, but they are all quite similar in construction. The table in Plate 10 is a rather typical example.

This type of table is quite difficult to date with any degree of accuracy, especially since the detachable top is so easy to replace. In attempting to date one, we must rely upon the general signs of age as discussed in Chapter 9, with particular attention to the hinges connecting the lid to the box and the manner in which the hinges themselves are fastened.

Stands

In view of the many sizes and shapes of the small table-like pieces of furniture called "stands" (usually for want of a better name), we have divided this general heading into two sub-headings, "wash stands" and "candle stands."

Wash Stands

As indicated, this term is completely arbitrary, and no doubt many of the pieces that fit the following description never held a pitcher and bowl. The type of wash stand most often encountered in the Pennsylvania countryside is quite similar in size and shape to the small tavern table described above, but with several important differences. The wash stand is normally about 23 inches high and unlike the small tavern table, usually has stretchers placed 6 or 8 inches from the floor. In addition to giving the table extra strength, the stretchers also serve to support a shelf. The wash stand may or may not have a low gallery around three sides of the top, as does the example shown in Plate 11, but it almost invariably has a drawer, sometimes two, located in the apron just below the top. The details of the drawer's construction and the presence or absence of pins in the leg joints are the best indicators of age in this type of stand. Both of these construction details are discussed in Chapter 9.

There are many variations of this basic type of stand. Some, made to fit into a corner, have only three legs; some have a large hole cut out of the top to receive the bottom of a wash bowl; some contain a small drawer below the shelf, and some late ones have turned towel bars built out from the ends (see Plate 12). Wash stands were constructed of almost every native Pennsylvania cabinet wood, although walnut and cherry were the most favored.

Candle Stands

The variety of candle stands is legion. They were made in all the sizes and shapes that the fertile minds of the cabinetmakers or farmers could invent. Again we can divide this type of furniture into two general categories: those

11. Wash stand, Maple, Circa 1845
Courtesy of Mr. and Mrs. John H. Coulter   *Photograph by Charles R. Steitz, Jr.*

12. Wash stand, Maple, Circa 1860
Courtesy of Mr. and Mrs. Stephen Palmer   *Photograph by Charles R. Steitz, Jr.*

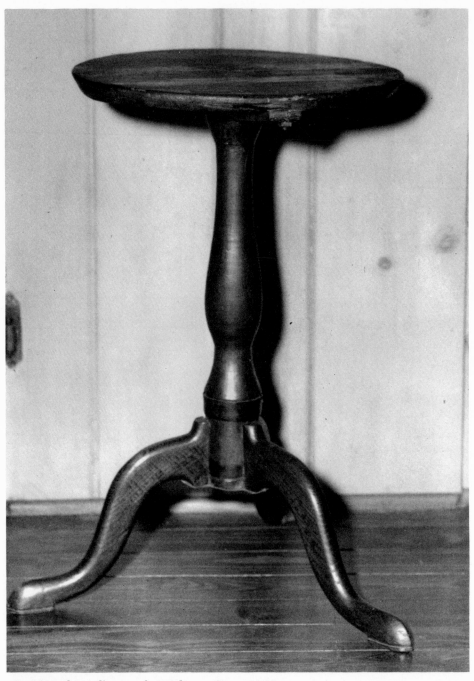

13. Tripod candle stand, Walnut, Circa 1790

Courtesy of Mr. David King   *Photograph by Charles R. Steitz, Jr.*

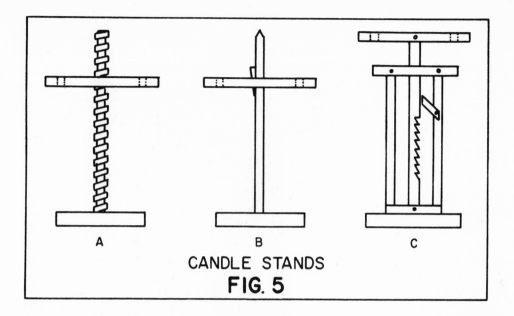

A   B   C

CANDLE STANDS
FIG. 5

with a flat surface on which to set a candleholder and those with the candle-holders built as an integral part of the stand.

The former category includes the familiar tripod stand with a turned shaft surmounted by a top (see Plate 13). The top may be of any shape or size and may be flat or dished. The dished top (or "pie crust") stand was a favorite product of the urban cabinetmakers but is rare in the country areas. The top may be stationary or built to allow it to tilt or—less frequently in the country—to tilt and twirl. The wood most commonly associated with this type of stand is mahogany, but the rural cabinetmakers also used native hardwoods such as walnut and cherry.

Stands in the second category are known as cobblers' stands, but their use was certainly not restricted to shoemakers. They all contained only three basic parts: a base, a shaft, and a device for holding the candles. But the design of these parts varied widely from stand to stand. The base might have three or four legs extending below it, or it might be a simple criss-crossing of two boards or have any one of a dozen other designs. The shafts were similar only in that they all permitted the candles to be raised or lowered. They were of three basic types (see Figure 5). The first type (A) was threaded and equipped with a crossarm which carried one or two candles. The crossarm could be raised or lowered by rotating it on the shaft. The second type (B) has an unthreaded shaft. On this one the crossarm is held in position by a wedge which is inserted through the oversized hole in the arm and allowed to bind against the shaft. The third type

14. The Tavern Kitchen of The Pennsylvania Farm Museum of Landis Valley. Notice the candle stand with its notched shaft.

Courtesy of the museum   *Photograph by Charles R. Steitz, Jr.*

(C) has a notched shaft, or ratchet, which is engaged and held in place by a pawl mounted on the frame of the stand. Note the candle stand in Plate 14.

Once in a while a stand is seen which has both a flat top to hold a candlestick and an adjustable crossarm for additional candles. But these are unusual and when found can be attributed to the ingenuity of an individual craftsman.

44

CHAPTER TWO

CHESTS AND BOXES

———————

As mentioned in the preceding chapter, the furniture brought by the early settlers to the New World consisted almost entirely of the chests and boxes into
which their few possessions were packed. The settlers were not long on these
shores before they began accumulating more goods, which meant that more
chests and boxes were required. Thus the production of these articles in America
probably began as early as the production of tables. It is not, however, within
the scope of this book to discuss in detail the earliest chests known in Pennsylvania, since those that have survived are in museums or private collections. If
the reader is interested in the earlier chests, or for that matter in any furniture
that antedates the middle of the eighteenth century, Wallace Nutting's *Furniture
Treasury* can be recommended as the best reference available today.

The better examples of simple chests (that is, chests without drawers) are
almost all made of six wide boards, with bracket feet and dovetailed corners—
which description would apply equally well to many seventeenth, eighteenth,
or early nineteenth century chests. Since there was so little change in style over
the years, any attempt to date a particular chest must be based almost entirely
on its hardware and the general signs of age. Because of the ease with which
hardware can be changed, dating by it alone can be a risky business indeed.
The first rule, then, is to be sure that the hardware is original. This can be
determined by looking for marks on the wood left by earlier hardware and by
examining the manner in which the present hardware is attached. There are
more detailed discussions of this subject in Chapters 9 and 10.

When we speak of hardware on chests and boxes, we are referring to the
hinges, locks, escutcheons, and if the chest is equipped with drawers, the pulls.
The escutcheons and pulls are considered to be hardware regardless of the material from which they were made (brass, porcelain, wood, etc.).

Generally speaking, the earliest chests with which we are concerned are those equipped with strap hinges, and since we are talking about Pennsylvania chests, these hinges are usually of the type that today are considered decorative. The presence of cotter pin hinges on a chest or box would normally indicate a date earlier than the period which we are studying, but since we so often are dealing with survival pieces, we should also keep in mind that this type of hinge is occasionally found on chests made as late as 1800 and on small boxes made until about 1820. Even though cotter pin hinges were used until these relatively late dates, the fragile nature of the hinge makes it quite rare today, and a piece still carrying its original set should be treated with some respect.

The cast-iron butt hinge came into general use in about 1830, at about the same time that screw-making machinery was invented. This combination proved too convenient and too inexpensive to be ignored, and so we find it on almost every chest and box made from that time until the cast-iron hinge gave way to the modern rolled-steel hinge early in the twentieth century.

There are two types of locks found on chests. The "box" type has a pierced keeper so attached to the lid of the chest that it drops into a hole in the top of the lock proper, where it can be engaged by the bolt. The "crab" lock gets its name from two curved pieces of metal, somewhat resembling the claws of a crab, which engage an arrowhead-shaped keeper mounted on the inside of the lid. A chest equipped with the former type can be locked only by turning the key, but the keeper of the latter type drops between the spring-held claws and locks the chest automatically. The crab lock can be quite hazardous when there are small children in the home, since it is possible for a child to crawl into a chest and be locked inside when the lid falls. It is a wise precaution, therefore, to wedge the exposed claws firmly open with a small block of wood, to prevent just such an accident. If the claws are enclosed within the body of the lock instead of exposed on top of it, some method must be devised to prevent the lid from closing completely or to stop the keeper from dropping all the way into the lock. Precautions of this nature can also prevent possible mutilation of the lock, or of the chest itself, should the key be lost or inadvertently locked inside. That this has happened many times is evidenced by the very few chests that are found in good condition, with crab lock and keeper still intact.

Because of its applicability to more than one type of furniture, hardware of various kinds will be described more fully in Chapter 10.

Chests

As defined by Nutting, a chest is "a receptacle with a lid, and generally a small till at one end. It may have no drawers, or one, two, and rarely three

15. Small blanket chest, Pine, Circa 1830. Notice irregular dovetails and the
wear on the bracket feet.   *Photograph by Charles R. Steitz, Jr.*

drawers." They can be found in all sizes, ranging from about 17 by 33 by 20
inches, like the one shown in Plate 15, to about 24 by 49 by 32 inches, like
the one in Plate 16. Most Pennsylvania chests were built without drawers,
although some do have two or three drawers across the bottom (again see Plate
16). One-drawer Pennsylvania chests, on the other hand, are quite unusual.
Often a chest is found with a "secret" compartment built below a false bottom in
the till. This compartment is usually reached by lifting the side of the till and
may or may not contain a concealed drawer or two.

The example in Plate 17 is shown primarily for its hinges, which are quite
representative of its period. This chest apparently was made with bracket feet

47

16. Large blanket chest, Pine, Circa 1820
Courtesy of Mr. and Mrs. Stephen Palmer   *Photograph by Charles R. Steitz, Jr.*

that seem to have been partially removed at one time or another, as it is unlikely that natural wear could have reduced them so far.

The chest in Plate 18 has a handle at each end and has never had feet of any kind, which indicates that, in spite of its size, it was probably intended for use as a sea chest. The handles on this particular chest and the nails with which they are attached are of hand-forged iron.

The chest pictured in Plate 19 is representative of a style made from about 1830 until about 1900. This style was very popular in rural Pennsylvania, and hardly a country sale goes by without one or two of them falling under the hammer. Because they are plentiful, these chests can still be purchased quite reasonably and can be used to provide excellent storage space, even in today's modern home.

The great majority of Pennsylvania chests made throughout the period we are discussing were of pine or poplar (tulipwood). Occasionally, though, a prized

48

17. Blanket chest showing strap hinges, Poplar, Circa 1830. Notice marks left by the label and wear caused by the corner of the till top.

Photograph by Charles R. Steitz, Jr.

example is found in walnut or cherry, either of which could be considered the most beautiful of our native cabinet woods.

The flat surfaces of a chest gave the itinerant artist or the yeoman with talent (real or fancied) a fine place to display his art. This was particularly true with regard to the Pennsylvania Dutch, whose love of color led them to decorate much of their furniture. The artist usually confined his efforts to the front of the chest, dividing the decoration into two or three panels and repeating each motif at least once. Needless to say, the presence of such original decoration on a chest today makes it considerably more valuable than a similar, but undecorated one. Of additional interest is the fact that the county of origin of a decorated chest can be determined by the decorative motif. A chest decorated

18. Sea chest, Pine, Circa 1820.   *Photograph by Charles R. Steitz, Jr.*

19. Late blanket chest, Pine, Circa 1860
Courtesy of Mr. David King   *Photograph by Charles R. Steitz, Jr.*

20. Single woodbox, Pine, Circa 1860. Rough, as found. Notice the wear on top edge of the front.

Courtesy of Mr. and Mrs. C. W. Bretz   *Photograph by Charles R. Steitz, Jr.*

with unicorns and/or horsemen would have been made in Berks County, while one with geometric designs such as stylized flowers (created with a compass) would be from Montgomery County; and one with an almost architectural feeling of sunken arched panels with a tulip or bird motif would be of Lancaster County provenance. The chests that bore initials or large printed names on the front were probably meant to be dower or hope chests.

Many decorated chests were signed by the artist. When the period of the artist's work is known, his signature provides an excellent clue to the age of chests showing similar details of construction and craftsmanship. A few of the artists, such as Christian Seltzer of Jonestown, who worked during the last quarter of the eighteenth century, have become quite famous. Any hitherto undiscovered example of his work would be quite a windfall today.

Woodboxes

A woodbox frequently resembles a chest in size and shape, but there the similarity ends. It was intended to be a strictly functional, not decorative, piece of furniture, and was usually built with much less care and craftsmanship than chests of the same period. As its name implies, this piece of furniture was used to hold a supply of firewood, usually in a spot convenient to the hearth. Woodboxes can be found in two distinct varieties: single as in Plate 20 and double

51

21. Double woodbox, Pine, Circa 1860
Courtesy of Mr. and Mrs. James T. Grove   *Photograph by Charles R. Steitz, Jr.*

as in Plate 21. The double box usually has one large compartment for firewood and a smaller one for kindling, although they are sometimes found with two equally-sized compartments. Individual need occasionally dictated modifications such as the woodbox with a back shown in Plate 22. Some woodboxes were built with dovetailed corners, but most were simply nailed together, and the type of nail used can provide a clue to the age of a particular box (see Chapter 10).

A woodbox differs from a chest in three additional ways: it never has a lock, it never has a till, and the lid, usually devoid of molding, is hinged at the back to a stationary section of the top, which extends two or three inches forward from the back of the box. This latter characteristic allows the lid to stay up when lifted, even though the box is placed flush against a wall. The inside of a woodbox invariably shows scars made by the hundreds of lengths of firewood that have been dropped into it, and the top edge of the front is frequently worn into a deep curve from the same treatment (see Plate 19). Most of the examples that we find today are of rather late vintage, since the early soft pine or poplar woodboxes could not withstand that kind of abuse for many years.

Bride's Boxes

The bride's box is frequently a miniature chest, complete in every detail down to the dovetailed corners and the little till. Tradition has it that these tiny chests were made by prospective bridegrooms for presentation to their intended brides, who would use them to store sewing equipment or trinkets. Examination of a number of bride's boxes tends to support this theory, chiefly because of the wide variance in the quality of workmanship from one box to another. There still exist, however, enough really good examples to suggest that the young man with little or no skill at cabinetmaking could purchase one, ready-made, from someone more expert than he.

Many of these little chests are equipped with removable trays, as is the one in Plate 23, which make them excellent jewelry or trinket boxes for today's bride.

22. Sitting room of the 1815 House of The Pennsylvania Farm Museum of
Landis Valley. Notice the woodbox with a back, the rod-back Windsor, and
the balloon-back rocker.

Courtesy of the museum   *Photograph by Charles R. Steitz, Jr.*

23. Bride's box, Pine, Circa 1820   *Photograph by Charles R. Steitz, Jr.*

24. Counter-top desk box, Pine, Circa 1860. Rough, as found.

Photograph by Charles R. Steitz, Jr.

Counter Top Desk Boxes

The counter top desk boxes that are occasionally discovered in the country are, in reality, throwbacks to a much earlier type of furniture. More than just survival examples of an earlier style, they actually skip back over several stages of desk evolution to be re-created very much in the likeness of their ancestors. The early desk box (which later evolved into the desk-on-frame) was resurrected to fill a need of the storekeepers of the era under discussion. These desk boxes were usually of pine or poplar and were built to be placed on the counter of a store and serve the proprietor as a writing surface as well as a repository for his records. They were simply wide boxes with dovetailed corners and slanted lids, quite similar in shape to a schoolmaster's desk, minus its legs (see Plate 24). Most desk boxes had a lip at the lower edge of the lid which served as a book rest. The inside of the box sometimes had a row of pigeon holes, but just as often it was left perfectly plain.

The most practical use we have seen for a counter top desk box in today's home is as a desk in the kitchen. The one that we saw is supported by a low shelf mounted on extra-large brackets; it is used to hold the usual conglomeration of grocery lists, cookbooks, and recipes.

Candle Boxes

Although not properly pieces of furniture, we feel that candle boxes were of sufficient importance in our early households to warrant their inclusion in this chapter. They can be found in many styles and in several woods, but those most

25. Candle box, Pine, Circa 1800. Pegged throughout.

Photograph by Charles R. Steitz, Jr.

often seen are narrow pine boxes, about 18 inches long by 9 inches wide, with a lid made to slide in grooves cut into the sides of the box (see Plate 25). Since they were made to hold the family's supply of good wax candles, an expensive item, they were frequently quite well constructed, often decorated, and occasionally even carved. The nice part of owning a candle box today is that it can still be used just as its maker intended. Most people, especially those who live in the country, keep a few candles about the house to supply light in the event of a power failure, and a candle box provides the perfect place to store them.

CHAPTER THREE

DESKS AND CHESTS OF DRAWERS

This chapter will be devoted, for the most part, to the furniture known to the trade as "case pieces." Since this term is frequently misunderstood, it would seem that a definition is in order. Webster defines "case" as "a box, sheath or covering," and this is the meaning that collectors and dealers wish to convey when they speak of a case piece. The case is the "box, sheath or covering" that surrounds the frame of a bureau, desk, cupboard, or chest of drawers—thus these are the case pieces. This leads to another definition, this time of "bureau," but unfortunately the definition is not quite as straightforward. Turning again to Webster we find that he defines "bureau" in two ways: as it is used in England, it means "a writing desk or table with drawers," and as used in the United States, "a chest of drawers, usually low and with a mirror." This is confusing enough, but confusion is compounded by the definition, again Webster's, of "dresser" as "a cupboard to hold dishes and cooking utensils" and again "a chest of drawers or bureau, with a mirror." In view of all this, we submit that the case pieces discussed in this book will be defined as follows:

Bureau desk   A writing desk with drawers and a slant top (See Plate 32).

Dresser   A cupboard used to hold dishes and cooking utensils and designed to stand along a wall, not in a corner (see Plates 36 and 37).

Chest of drawers   A chest without a lifting lid, composed entirely of drawers. It can be low as in Plate 27, or high as in Plate 29.

If the reader will accept these definitions, we can direct our attention to the furniture itself.

Chests of Drawers

There is little doubt that the chest of drawers is the result of logical evolution from the simple chest. The steps are quite obvious because we can still see many chests with no drawers, a goodly number with one stratum of drawers at the bottom, and—still available though not so abundant—some with two strata of drawers. With the advent of three-drawer chests, the hinged lid was replaced by a fixed top, and the chest of drawers as we know it was created.

Although low chests of drawers are known to have been made in this country from late in the seventeenth century until the present, we believe that they were practically nonexistent in the rural areas until well into the nineteenth century. This theory was derived from consideration of two salient points:

1) The few examples of low chests of drawers found in our rural areas and dated prior to 1820 almost always show style features and construction details of city-made furniture.

2) The fact that country people of the eighteenth century owned relatively few clothes, coupled with the fact that a large number of plain chests (without drawers) have been found in the rural areas, indicates that these people would have had little need for a chest of drawers. Having presented our arguments, we shall let the reader decide for himself whether or not this theory is valid.

The painted and decorated chests of drawers found in Pennsylvania Dutch country are of course the logical outgrowth of the painted and decorated chests of the same locale. As with the chests, an original decoration on a chest of drawers should be carefully preserved if at all possible.

Although we promised to discuss only antiques that are available to the average collector, we cannot pass this point without mentioning the rare and beautiful painted furniture that has come out of the Valley of the Mahatonga. Though much like other Pennsylvania Dutch furniture in construction, the decoration of Mahatonga Valley furniture places it in a class all its own. While the typical angel, flower, and bird motifs by which this furniture is recognized have been found on many different pieces, probably the most familiar are the chests of drawers, such as that in Plate 26, and the dressers, as in Plate 39. Needless to say, very few articles from this obscure valley have come to light, and those that have are highly prized.

Fortunately for those of us interested in country furniture, the rural Pennsylvania craftsmen did not accept the style change which favored solid ends in chests of drawers and led to so much splitting in eighteenth century furniture. Since the cabinetmakers continued to use the older stile and rail construction, many of the pieces that we find today have panelled ends that have remained intact through the years.

27. Low (cottage) chest of drawers, Pine, Circa 1860. Note the inset wooden escutcheons. *Photograph by Charles R. Steitz, Jr.*

A low chest of drawers usually has four full drawers as in Plate 27. Occasionally we see one with three full drawers and a top tier consisting of three small drawers (Plate 28). A tall one can have as many as six tiers with the top tier usually having three small drawers (Plate 29). The drawers may be all of the same depth, or graduated, with the deepest usually at the bottom. The drawers in both types were always dovetailed, and generally speaking, the larger the dovetails, the older the piece, as explained in Chapter 9.

Since we are dealing mainly with survival pieces, the rule that tool marks and construction features provide our most reliable clues to age is still applicable.

28. Bedroom of the 1815 House of The Pennsylvania Farm Museum of Landis Valley. Note the low chest of drawers and decorated balloon-back chair.
Courtesy of the museum   *Photograph by Charles R. Steitz, Jr.*

Hardware—and we include wooden knobs in this category—is a good indicator of age if we are sure that the original hardware is still on the piece. But this is a big "if." Pieces of any respectable age that still carry their original pulls are quite rare. This is due in part to the vulnerability of this type of hardware and in part to the ease with which a piece was "updated" by changing the old pulls to a style currently in vogue. When pulls have been changed to a later style, evidence of the older ones is usually quite easy to find. Often holes that have been neatly plugged on the outside will be readily visible from the inside of the drawer; or dents, the result of bails striking the wood as they fell, can be found

29. High chest in bedroom of the 1815 House of The Pennsylvania Farm
Museum of Landis Valley.

Courtesy of the museum

Photograph by Charles R. Steitz, Jr.

26. Pennsylvania Dutch (Mahatonga Valley) chest of drawers, Circa 1834
Courtesy of The Philadelphia Museum of Art: The A. H. Rice Collection
Photograph by A. J. Wyatt, Staff Photographer

on drawer fronts. It is not quite as easy to recognize new hardware that has replaced an older set of the same type. In order to do this we must rely on the appearance of the hardware itself, a subject which we shall take up in detail in Chapter 10.

The chest of drawers shown in Plate 27 is a rather typical low pine chest of its period. The inlaid maple escutcheons are an unusual feature which indicate that this piece was never intended to be painted.

30. Victorian high chest of drawers, Walnut, Circa 1870. Not of country origin, but frequently found in rural areas.

Courtesy of Mr. and Mrs. T. Gamon, III   *Photograph by Charles R. Steitz, Jr.*

31. Late Victorian chest of drawers. Rough as found.

Photograph by Charles R. Steitz, Jr.

The examples shown in Plates 30 and 31 are of the late Victorian style favored by country folk around 1860. Although they should properly be classed as city pieces, many are found at country auctions and they are representative of the general degeneration of taste in furniture that started at that time and has never really ended.

Bureau Desks

The bureau desk evolved in a manner similar to that of the chest of drawers, but in the opposite direction. While the addition of drawers in a chest of drawers

32. Hepplewhite bureau desk, Cherry, Circa 1790. Certainly not of country origin, but long located in rural Lancaster County.
Courtesy of Mr. and Mrs. Thomas Garber   *Photograph by Charles R. Steitz, Jr.*

started from the bottom and went up, the pattern in the desk was from the top down. As mentioned in the previous chapter, the first desks in this country were simply desk boxes, which were subsequently mounted on frames to become desks-on-frames. The next step was to build a drawer in the top of the frame and then to make the frame and box as one piece. Thus, early in the eighteenth century the evolution of the bureau desk was complete. This evolution was given impetus about 1700, when someone realized that a writing surface could be provided, along with sufficient leg room, if the lid were hinged to open downward instead of upward.

The bureau desk is relatively scarce throughout the Pennsylvania countryside, and when one is encountered, it can be suspected of having been made in a city and transported to the country. The one pictured in Plate 32 is a fine specimen that has been in rural Lancaster County for several generations but was probably made in Philadelphia or Lancaster.

33. Schoolmaster's desk, Pine, Circa 1845
Courtesy of Mr. and Mrs. Stephen Palmer   *Photograph by Charles R. Steitz, Jr.*

Schoolmaster's Desks

The only type of antique desk found in any quantity in rural Pennsylvania is the so-called "schoolmaster's" desk, a furniture style that is not merely a survival example of an earlier style, but in fact an anachronism. The one shown in Plate 33 was made in about 1850, almost a century and a half after cabinet-makers discovered the advantage of hinging desk lids at the bottom.

66

Since the lids of schoolmaster's desks were hinged at the top, the writing surface had to be the top of the lid; however, on most of these desks the top is too high to provide a comfortable writing surface when the writer is seated in a normal chair. Moreover, many examples have boxes so deep that it is impossible to get one's knees underneath them. Thus, it seems to us that in most cases the schoolmaster's desk, in addition to being a throwback, was not a desk at all, but a sort of lectern, behind which the master stood, peering down at his young charges from his awesome, adult height. In fact, many of these desks never saw the inside of a school at all, but were used by shopkeepers or bookkeepers as high work tables, at which they could stand to work on their accounts.

Commodes

Again we have arrived at a point at which a definition is necessary. The words "wash stand" and "commode" have come to be used almost interchangeably, so in an effort to differentiate between the two, we again turn to Webster. He defines "commode" as "a movable sink or washstand, with a closet," and we have seized upon the word "closet" to indicate the difference. A commode, then, is a case piece somewhat similar to a small chest of drawers, but containing only one, or occasionally two drawers just under the top, with the rest of the piece (where the lower drawers would be in a chest of drawers) taken up by a

34. Commode, Pine and Walnut, Circa 1830

Photograph by Charles R. Steitz, Jr.

67

35. Lift-top commode, Pine, Circa 1860
Courtesy of Mr. and Mrs. J. V. James   *Photograph by Bowen Studio*

cupboard, or "closet," usually with a single door. A wash stand, as described in Chapter 1, is not a case piece, but a stand, and as such it has no closet beneath the drawer. Please note that we are not talking about the factory-made oak or chestnut commodes that formed a part of every bedroom "suite" made in the late Victorian period.

The commode was made from about 1825 until modern plumbing rendered it obsolete. It is again in great demand because today's housewife has found it a versatile piece of furniture, useful in many ways and in every room in the house. The piece in Plate 34 is a rather typical example. It should be noted, however, that the present owner found the commode in Plate 34 lacking its original towel bar and had a low gallery placed at the back of the piece's top.

Another type of commode occasionally found in Pennsylvania, but more typically in New England, is the lift-top commode pictured in Plate 35. Instead of having a closet in which to store the pitcher and bowl, this type has a sort of hutch under its hinged lid and a drawer or very small closet below. In many ways the lift-top commode was probably the more convenient of the two types.

CHAPTER FOUR

CUPBOARDS

———

Pennsylvania's country cabinetmakers made their greatest contribution to our furniture heritage in the design and construction of large case pieces, an achievement largely forced upon them by the prevalence of stone farmhouses in Pennsylvania. These homes did not readily lend themselves to closets, so in an effort to solve their storage problem, the people who lived in them developed a variety of cupboards to hold their dishes, preserves, cooking utensils, and clothing. Among the styles built were some that were similar in design to cupboards produced in other parts of the country and a few that were unique to Pennsylvania. Those that can be considered unique to this state were the Lancaster and Montgomery County jelly cupboards, the Dutch cupboard, and the milk cupboard. These will all be covered in detail in this chapter.

There was a time when a cupboard was exactly what the name implied, a board used to hold cups, but by the beginning of the span of years we are covering, the cupboard had developed into a major piece of home furnishing. To indicate the steps in this development, we direct the reader's attention to the cupboard shown in Plate 36. This early pewter cupboard was the forerunner of several later types, the names of which are household words today. It can be seen that only the addition of doors to the bottom section is needed to convert this piece into a Welsh dresser, after which glass-panelled doors added to the top section would make it a Dutch cupboard. (Note: the adjectives "Welsh" and "Dutch" are used here in the manner which has grown up through popular usage. A true Welsh dresser would be of carved oak, and the frame of the top section would be scrolled in a distinctive pattern of scalloping.)

Welsh Dressers

In attempting to explain why the Welsh dresser is called a dresser rather than a cupboard, we find that "dresser" is derived from the French *dressoir*,

36. Pewter cupboard, Pine, Circa 1750   *Photograph by Charles R. Steitz, Jr.*

which is defined as "a bench on which something, as meat, is dressed." This of course gets us nowhere, so we can only say that "dresser" is the proper term for this type of furniture and hope the reader will accept it on faith.

The Welsh dresser is really composed of two cupboards, an open one on top and a deeper closed one below (see Plate 37). They were almost always made in two pieces, with tenons on the sides of the top section fitting into mortices in the top of the base. The shelves in both sections are always stationary and are usually morticed into the sides. Dressers (and cupboards) made in Pennsylvania usually have slots cut into one or more of the shelves of the top section for the display of spoons. The shelves of the top section usually have two parallel grooves, cut near the back, along their entire length. These grooves were used to hold the rims of plates that were displayed at the back of the dresser, thus preventing the plates from sliding forward. Another feature of Welsh dressers, particularly those of Pennsylvania provenance, is the guard rail located above each shelf of the top section to prevent the dishes displayed thereon from tumbling from the dresser.

As is to be expected, Welsh dressers were made in all the native cabinet woods, but those made from walnut or cherry are the most highly prized today.

Most of the cupboards discussed in this book, including the Welsh dresser, were made throughout the span of years we are discussing. Consequently, any attempt to date a particular cupboard or dresser must be based on a thorough consideration of all of the signs of age discussed in Chapters 9 and 10.

Dutch Cupboards

Almost everything that has been said regarding the Welsh dresser also applies to the Dutch cupboard, except that the upper section of the latter is enclosed by small paned glass doors (Plate 38). These doors of course eliminate the scalloping around the top section and the need for guard rails above the shelves. Since this type is considered less desirable than the Welsh dresser, many a piece that started out as an honest Dutch cupboard has been converted into a spurious Welsh dresser by a few simple expedients—the removal of the doors and door frames, the judicious use of a scroll saw, and the addition of guard rails.

When properly made, the horizontal mullions of the doors in the top section of a Dutch cupboard will be directly in front of the shelves and will not interfere with a view of the contents of the cupboard. The sides and back-boards of the top section usually extend 6 to 8 inches below the upper doors, thus allowing a usable space between the top and bottom sections. If this space is much less than 6 inches high, there is a good chance that the cupboard has been cut down, probably to fit into a room with a low ceiling.

37. Welsh dresser, Pine, Circa 1790

Courtesy of Mr. David King

Photograph by Charles R. Steitz, Jr.

38. Dutch cupboard, Pine, Circa 1840

Courtesy of Mr. and Mrs. Edward C. Shaw   *Photograph by Charles R. Steitz, Jr.*

73

39. Pennsylvania Dutch (Mahatonga Valley) dresser (Dutch cupboard), Circa
1834
Courtesy of The Philadelphia Museum of Art: The Titus C. Gessey Collection
Photograph by A. J. Wyatt, Staff Photographer

    Most of the Dutch cupboards encountered today were made after 1830.
These pieces were originally painted, and when found today they can be
carrying from three to twelve coats of paint—a true challenge to the amateur
refinisher.

Kitchen Cupboards

This modification of the Dutch cupboard came into vogue about 1890. In construction it is much like the Dutch cupboard, with two doors and two drawers in the lower section and two doors in the upper section. The principal difference is that the doors in the upper section are made with wooden panels rather than glass. The bottom section was sometimes made as a dry sink (see Chapter 7), with the usual zinc-lined well. This construction technique has given the name "high sink" to all cupboards of this type, but since many were made without the sink and all of these pieces were designed specifically for the kitchen, we feel that the name "kitchen cupboard" is more appropriate.

Occasionally someone will try to make one of these late pieces look like a Dutch cupboard, but the modification is usually quite obvious. The modifier seldom goes to the trouble of morticing the mullions into the stiles and rails of the doors, and there is invariably a conspicuous absence of the usual signs of age, such as wooden pins in the door joints, old hardware, and old glass.

These cupboards, too, were originally meant to be painted and consequently are found chiefly in pine or poplar or in a combination of these and other woods such as maple, chestnut, or oak.

Jelly Cupboards

In addition to the large two-piece cupboards, Pennsylvania craftsmen produced many attractive and useful smaller cupboards, which were complete in one unit. These pieces have come to be called "jelly cupboards," and it is quite likely that each autumn found them well stocked with apple and grape jelly and various other preserves.

Two distinct varieties of this cupboard are known, the Montgomery County and the Lancaster County. The Montgomery County jelly cupboard is characterized by its simplicity, as is shown to good advantage by the example in Plate 41. With its four-panelled door and rather heavy cornice, this particular example is faintly reminiscent of the Dutch kas, though much reduced in size (58 inches high by 35 inches wide). The interior of a jelly cupboard has several stationary shelves, usually about 8 or 9 inches apart, with the lowest shelf set 11 or 12 inches from the bottom to allow for the storage of larger items. This type of cupboard is usually equipped with a wooden catch and is seldom, if ever, found with a lock. Although late examples are sometimes seen, the Montgomery County jelly cupboard is generally considered to be an older style than its Lancaster County counterpart.

Actually a survival example of an Empire sideboard, the Lancaster County jelly cupboard (see Plate 42) is somewhat more elaborate than its eastern cousin.

41. Montgomery County jelly cupboard, Pine, Circa 1840. Note normal wear on frame and unusual wear on door. *Photograph by Charles R. Steitz, Jr.*

42. Lancaster County jelly cupboard, Pine, Circa 1860

Photograph by Charles R. Steitz, Jr.

It has two drawers built just below its top, and the drawers and top are frequently built out so as to overhang the cupboard section in the Victorian manner. The cupboard, with its stationary shelves, generally has two panelled doors, which open outward from the center. The doors are most often secured by a metal catch, while the drawers frequently have locks set into their rounded fronts. The Lancaster County jelly cupboard is usually found in pine or poplar (originally painted) and dates from about 1840 to 1895.

Milk Cupboards

As far as we can determine, the milk cupboard is another piece purely of Pennsylvania provenance. It is large, of single-unit construction, and characterized by upper and lower doors of equal size. The upper doors and lower doors are separated by two side-by-side drawers leaving no space between the upper and lower sections. Both sections are of equal depth.

These cupboards are most often found in pine or poplar, with wooden drawer pulls and latches and cast-iron butt hinges. They were made from approximately 1830 until about 1880.

43. Pie cupboard, Pine and Tin, Circa 1860
Courtesy of The Mercer Museum, Doylestown, Pennsylvania   Photograph by Charles R. Steitz, Jr.

Pie Cupboards

The so-called "pie cupboard," or "pie safe," deviates considerably from the pieces we have discussed in that it is panelled in tin rather than wood (see Plate 43). Probably a late derivation of the early livery cupboard, this unusual piece was used to keep food (perhaps even pies) out of the reach of mice and other pests. The tin was perforated with hundreds of small holes, usually arranged in a pleasing geometric or floral design, which allowed air to circulate over the food stored within and thus retard spoilage.

Although they were usually mounted on legs, pie safes were occasionally suspended from the ceiling as a further safeguard against mice. This is indicated by ring bolts or large screw eyes set into the top. Pie safes were made from the middle of the nineteenth until the beginning of the twentieth century, and some are still used in a few Pennsylvania Dutch sections of the state where electricity is culturally acceptable in the barn, but not in the house. Very late examples are found with wire screening replacing the tin.

Wardrobes

Although not cupboards in the true sense of the word, wardrobes are large case pieces quite similar to cupboards in construction (see Plate 44). They served the same purpose as the Dutch kas, and though made much later than the era of the kas, many still carry features reminiscent of those earlier pieces. As mentioned earlier, Pennsylvania farmhouses were built without closets, so the kas and later the wardrobe probably were used to silence many a hausfrau's complaints about clothes hanging from wall pegs. Incidentally, this problem still exists in many of the same farmhouses, and the same remedy is available to anyone restoring one of them.

The wardrobe was always constructed in one unit, with one or two long doors set well in from the sides and well up from the bottom. It differs from other cupboards chiefly in its lack of shelves. Below the doors there is almost always a tier of drawers, the number of drawers equalling the number of doors above. The ends of a particular piece might or might not be panelled, but the doors invariably are. The wardrobe usually stands on bracket feet of one type or another, and like the kas, usually has a rather heavy mold around the top. Inside, just under the top, a bar for holding hangers extends from one side to the other.

Wardrobes are found in pine, poplar, walnut, and cherry, and their construction spans the entire period we are studying. As with most cupboards, any attempt at dating must be based on close examination of the hardware and careful attention to the general signs of age.

Corner Cupboards

Country corner cupboards are found in two basic styles: one strongly suggests the Welsh dresser, and the other has almost all the features of the Dutch cupboard. The major difference between these two pieces and a corner cupboard is, of course, that the corner cupboard is built on a triangular floor plan, which allows it to be placed into a corner of a room with no loss of floor space. It differs further from the Welsh dresser and the Dutch cupboard in that its upper and lower sections always have nearly the same depth, and the upper section generally rests flush atop the lower section, leaving no room for counter space.

Corner cupboards that were constructed as pieces of furniture, not as architectural components, were usually made in two sections. When this was the case, the lower section was set back about ¾ inch from the upper, which allowed a strip of molding to be fastened around the top edge of the lower section to hold the upper section in position. A cupboard of this type can have one or two doors below and one, two, or no doors above (see Plates 45 and 46). The lower doors

45. Corner cupboard, Pine, Circa 1800
Courtesy of Mr. David King   *Photograph by Charles R. Steitz, Jr.*

are always wooden and usually panelled, while the upper doors, when present, are usually of small-paned glass. Cupboards that have no upper doors are found with either plain or scalloped frames. The shelves can be plain, or they can have shaped and/or molded edges; they may be with or without slots for spoons. A corner cupboard may sit flush on the floor or be raised on low bracket or turned feet. If all this sounds as though almost endless combinations of features are found in corner cupboards, then our purpose is achieved. There are almost as many variations of these practical, space-saving cupboards as there were people who wanted them. As with any of the other cupboards, they were made in any available wood and over a long period of years, so dating again must be based on the general signs of age.

46. Corner of the Grossmutter House (Grandmother House) of The Pennsylvania Farm Museum of Landis Valley. Note corner cupboard and ladder-back chair.
Courtesy of the museum   *Photograph by Charles R. Steitz, Jr.*

44. Wardrobe, Pine, Circa 1850   *Photograph by Charles R. Steitz, Jr.*

40. Room 1151, Decorative Arts Wing, The Philadelphia Museum of Art. Note the Pennsylvania Dutch furniture: Dutch cupboard, bow-back Windsor armchair, balloon-back rocker, painted chest, hanging cupboard, settee, and crickets.

Courtesy of The Philadelphia Museum of Art   *Photograph by A. J. Wyatt, Staff Photographer*

Hanging Cupboards

Hanging cupboards were great favorites in early Pennsylvania and can be found in many sizes, shapes, and styles. They can be open or closed with wooden or glass-paned doors (see Plates 40 and 47). They can be composed entirely of small drawers, as were the spice cupboards, or they can have a combination of shelves and drawers.

47. Hanging cupboard, Pine, Circa 1810   *Photograph by Charles R. Steitz, Jr.*

Hanging cupboards seem to have been used in the old days for much the same reason that we might use them today—to keep small articles out of the reach of small hands, thus keeping the articles and the hands safe from harm.

84

CHAPTER FIVE

CHAIRS

The dearth of ready cash for luxuries, the lack of close communication with the style centers, and the relatively low value placed on physical comfort by country folk in general are all reflected in the chairs favored by our early rural Pennsylvanians. As is true of country folk the world over, their chairs were used primarily at the table, and not for relaxation. These generalizations are borne out by the almost total lack of pre-Victorian upholstered chairs found in our rural areas. Most of the chairs they did use were "turned" chairs, which were light enough to be drawn up to the table easily or lined in rows for worship, yet strong enough to hold the most portly occupant. The varieties of these chairs are legion, with their rush, cane, or plank seats and their dozens of different back shapes, but they all share the common characteristic of socket-joint construction.

Almost from the beginnings of our country, the chairmaker was a specialist, devoting his entire time to his trade and unhampered by competition from cabinetmakers or other artisans. When men untrained in the art tried their hands at chairmaking, as some occasionally did, the results were far from satisfactory, as is indicated by the few surviving chairs of this nature. So specialized was the trade of chairmaking that it was often passed down from father to son for many generations. In the mountains of our southern states, there exists today at least one establishment in which a chairmaker is still working at his trade, using the old methods and inherited tools and turning out ladder-back chairs almost exactly like those produced in the eighteenth century.

Ladder-back Chairs

The earliest style of chair belonging to the period under study is the ladder-back, or slat-back, chair (see Plate 48). This popular style was made in all parts of the country from about 1700 until the present and is still much in demand.

48. Ladder-back chair, Maple, Circa 1820   *Photograph by Charles R. Steitz, Jr.*

The chair was made with or without arms and usually with a rush or splint seat; the back was made with three to six slats (see Plate 46). Since they were made over such a long period of time and always with much the same methods, it is almost impossible to judge the age of a ladder-back by cursory examination, although wear at the proper points often enables us to make an educated guess (see Chapter 9 for a more detailed discussion).

While the slats of ladder-backs of all ages are morticed into the back posts, it is only on the earlier examples that we find them with the top slat held by a wooden pin through the post and the slat and with similar pins holding the arms (when present) to the front posts. These pins make the restoration of an early ladder-back a job for an expert, since thorough restoration of any turned chair includes re-gluing, which, when done properly, requires taking the chair completely apart. When a chair *is* taken apart, the presence or absence of pod-bit holes (again see Chapter 9) can give another good indication of its age.

Many of the old ladder-backs have suffered excessive wear on the ends of their legs. A chair that has lost 2 or 3 inches of its height is an impractical buy for every-day use, since the replacement of this much leg constitutes major and expensive restoration.

While the better examples of ladder-backs have bold, deeply turned front stretchers, this is a style feature characteristic of city-made pieces and seldom found on country examples.

Windsor Chairs

Although originally an English design, the Windsor chair was made in America as early as 1720. The first American Windsors were made in Philadelphia, where a style recognizably different from the British took shape. Windsors made in England had little or no rake to their legs and frequently had a central back splat, usually pierce and/or scroll decorated. American examples, on the other hand, had decidedly raked legs and seldom if ever had a back splat.

Good early Windsors were made with seats about 1½ inch thick, deeply saddled to accommodate the sitter. Leg sockets were frequently drilled completely through the seat and a wooden wedge inserted into the end grain of the leg, fastening the leg into the seat much as an ax handle is wedged tight into its head. That this made an extremely strong joint is evidenced by the number of Windsors still serviceable after some two hundred years of use.

Early Pennsylvania Windsors are readily recognizable by their distinctive leg turnings, which are decidedly different from those of contemporary New England chairs (see Plate 52 and Figure 6). The turning on the legs of later Windsors from all sections of the country tends to be in the less ornate "bamboo" pattern.

Although Windsors were introduced into this country in Philadelphia, their use and production does not seem to have spread to any great extent into the rural areas of the state. Of the nine types listed by Thomas Ormsbee in his *Field Guide to Early American Furniture,* only the rod-back (or Sheraton Windsor), the loop-back and the firehouse Windsor can be found in any quantity outside of Philadelphia, and these are usually late, factory-made examples.

49. One of a pair of Sheraton Windsor (arrow-back) armchairs by Wm. Lee, who worked in New York around 1840. Chairs found in eastern Pennsylvania.

Photograph by Charles R. Steitz, Jr.

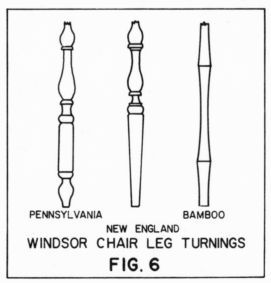

PENNSYLVANIA   BAMBOO

NEW ENGLAND

WINDSOR CHAIR LEG TURNINGS

FIG. 6

50. Entry hall in the DeCosta House, Philadelphia, Pa.

Photograph courtesy of The Philadelphia Museum of Art

51. Rod-Back or Sheraton Windsor, Circa 1820

Courtesy of Mr. and Mrs. Philip Gehret   *Photograph by Charles R. Steitz, Jr.*

These chairs, made of dissimilar woods, were always painted, not finished in the natural wood as is the vogue today. The most common colors were dark green, dark blue, black, and, somewhat surprisingly, white, as well as a simulated rosewood graining of black over a base of red.

Since we can add nothing to the subject of Windsor chairs that has not been covered by Ormsbee in his excellent volume *The Windsor Chair,* we will

52. Tavern Kitchen of The Pennsylvania Farm Museum of Landis Valley. Note Dutch cupboard, one end of a large farm table, and Sheraton (left) and loop-back Windsor chairs.

Courtesy of the museum   *Photograph by Charles R. Steitz, Jr.*

close the subject by calling the reader's attention to Plates 49, 50, 51, 52 and 53, which illustrate the three styles mentioned above.

53. Firehouse Windsor, Circa 1850   *Photograph by Charles R. Steitz, Jr.*

Plank-bottom Chairs

The plank-bottom—or kitchen Windsor, as it is sometimes called—is a direct descendant of the more elegant Philadelphia Windsor, and it was in the decoration of these chairs that the Pennsylvania Dutch artists came into their own (see Plate 54). A factory-made product from its inception in about 1830,

54. Plank-bottom chair, Circa 1860   *Photograph by Charles R. Steitz, Jr.*

these chairs gained wide acceptance among the Pennsylvania Dutch, who bought them unfinished and quickly transformed them into the colorful "fancy chairs" that they loved. The wide crest slat was a natural place for their beloved bird or floral decorations, while the back posts and the front seat roll were treated with the typical geometric or stylized leaf and vine designs. Even the legs and rungs received their share of the decoration, usually in the form of rings painted

93

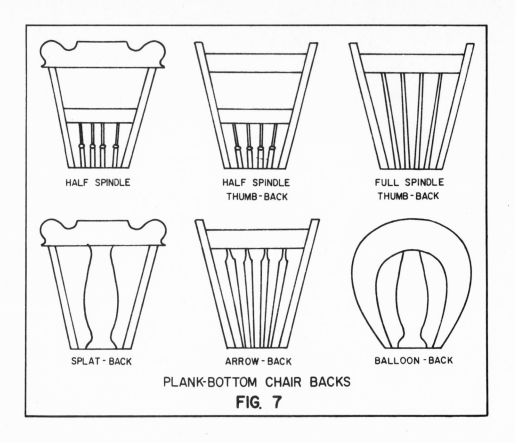

HALF SPINDLE

HALF SPINDLE
THUMB-BACK

FULL SPINDLE
THUMB-BACK

SPLAT-BACK

ARROW-BACK

BALLOON-BACK

PLANK-BOTTOM CHAIR BACKS
FIG. 7

around the turnings. The seat often had a stripe around the back and sides, about an inch in from the edge. Balloon-back and half spindle chairs (see Figure 7) were among the most favored by the Dutch because of the additional flat surfaces available for decoration.

The decoration was applied over a background paint such as dark green, dark blue, dark tan, brown, black, or yellow. When one of these chairs with its original decoration is encountered today, the background color, as well as the decorative detail, is seen to have mellowed to a degree almost impossible to imitate. Needless to say, every effort should be made to preserve the original decoration, but if this proves impractical the chair can be redecorated, using the old methods and materials. It is not the purpose of this book to delve into details of furniture decoration, but the reader interested in this subject will find several very informative books in the accompanying bibliography.

The seats of plank-bottom chairs, which were most often of pine, were not saddled like the seats of Windsors, but were scooped out across the width of the seat toward the back to a depth of about half of the total thickness of the plank. This simple treatment produced a remarkably comfortable chair.

The legs were connected to one another by single box stretchers, occasionally reinforced by an additional one in the front. The front stretcher, or stretchers, were usually lightly turned, but this turning is often completely worn away by the abrasive action of many dangling heels.

Old plank-bottoms can be used as kitchen chairs today equally as well as when they were new, or as dining room chairs in an informal setting, or as side chairs anywhere in the house. They are still being made, but few of today's manufacturers take the time or trouble to decorate their chairs in imitation of earlier models, since a natural wood finish is the current vogue.

Rockers

The same factories that made plank-bottom chairs also made rockers, often to match the chairs, and frequently sold sets of six side chairs and a matching rocker. These rocking chairs were made in two basic styles: the high-backed armchairs called Boston or Salem rockers, and a lower-backed chair without arms that has come to be called a nursing rocker (see Plate 55). The only dif-

55. Nursing rocker, Circa 1860
Courtesy of Dr. and Mrs. James G. Mackey   *Photograph by Charles R. Steitz, Jr.*

95

56. Boston rocker, Circa 1850
Courtesy of Mr. and Mrs. Charles Supplee   *Photograph by Charles R. Steitz, Jr.*

ference between Boston and Salem rockers is in the construction of their seats. The Boston rocker has a seat that curves up at the back, and down in the front while the seat of a Salem rocker is perfectly flat (see Plates 56 and 57). Both Boston and Salem rockers were often made with cherry arms, which, unlike the rest of the chair, were not intended to be painted. Balloon-back rockers (Plate 22) were popular, too.

96

57. Salem rocker, Circa 1865   *Photograph by Charles R. Steitz, Jr.*

58. Settee, Circa 1860

Courtesy of Mr. and Mrs. Robert Levison   *Photograph by Charles R. Steitz, Jr.*

Like plank-bottom chairs, rockers were also favorites of the Pennsylvania Dutch, and were decorated in much the same ways. They, too, were introduced in 1830 and are still being made today. Though these reproductions are factory decorated in an attempt to copy the old designs, they should not deceive anyone, since the new ones are obviously fresh and not done by hand.

The runners of very early rocking chairs were either the narrow "carpet cutter" kind, which were pegged into slots at the bottom of the legs, or broad, flat runners with sockets into which the legs were fastened. The runners we are accustomed to seeing today, which appear to be neither too narrow nor too broad, indicate a chair of rather recent vintage.

Settees

Another product of the factories that made plank-bottom chairs and rockers was the settee, or "deacon's bench." These were made to match the chairs and rockers but were seldom sold as part of a set. They were built with solid plank seats and in lengths ranging from 5 to 8 feet. They had either four or eight legs, and, like the chairs, were produced in a great variety of back styles—full and half-spindle, arrowback, etc. (see Plates 58 and 59).

98

59. Parlor of the 1815 House of The Pennsylvania Farm Museum of Landis Valley. Note the rod-back bamboo-turned settee.

Courtesy of the museum   *Photograph by Charles R. Steitz, Jr.*

Settees are becoming quite scarce and when found usually command good prices. Again, like the chairs and rockers, they were originally painted and decorated, and like the rockers, they were often made with cherry arms that remained unpainted in the original.

A hybrid achieved by combining a rocker and a settee is the "mammy's bench." This is nothing more than a short settee mounted on rockers and equipped with a removable fence extending from one arm (usually the right one) about halfway across the front of the seat. With the baby safely in place behind the fence, his mother could sit at the other end of the bench and keep her hands busy with chores while rocking Junior happily to sleep. There are, of course, fewer mammy's benches to be found than ordinary settees, but even more rare is the *double* mammy's bench, with two fences, one extending from either arm. We cannot quite imagine a woman lucky enough to busily engage in handwork and not have at least one of the children on either side of her wake up and demand her attention.

60. Wash bench, Circa 1880
Courtesy of Mr. and Mrs. James T. Grove   *Photograph by Charles R. Steitz, Jr.*

Wash Benches

Originally intended to be placed outside the back door to hold a wash bucket, wash benches also provided a fine place to sit. They were usually about 18 inches high and were of varying lengths, from about 4 to 12 feet. They were quite simple in construction, made much like the picnic benches produced today (see Plate 60). The better ones were made with the legs morticed completely through the seat (a double mortice for each leg) and with a narrow apron just below the seat. This apron, which was often lightly scrolled at each end, is frequently found on only one side of the bench. The reason for this becomes obvious when we remember that the bench was intended to be placed along a wall, so that only one side would show anyway. Similarly, a bench is sometimes found with one of its back corners rounded off and the other left square, indicating that the bench was made to be set into a corner. The legs of a wash bench were frequently braced, either diagonally to the center of the underside of the seat or straight across from leg to leg.

Since it was primarily intended for outdoor use, the wash bench was often heavily painted, but exposure to the weather for many years usually removed most or all of the paint. It is in this condition that we find most of them today. While they are still ideal for outdoor use, many people today prefer to refinish them in the natural wood, particularly the shorter benches, and use them in various places within the home.

The age of a wash bench can be quite difficult to determine, since the same style of bench was made for many, many years. Chapter 9 might prove helpful in establishing the approximate age of a particular piece.

100

61. Cricket (foot stool), Circa 1860   *Photograph by Charles R. Steitz, Jr.*

Foot Stools

The wooden foot stool, or cricket, is really just a miniature wash bench. The only differences are that the stool is always equipped with an apron on both sides, and that it is about one-fifteenth the size of a bench (see Plates 40 and 61).

The flat areas of a stool provided another fine place for decoration, which was often lavishly applied. Unfortunately, the type of wear to which a foot stool is subjected prevented most of them from coming down to us with their decoration intact. While we can often find vestiges of decoration, especially at the ends of a stool, the center design is usually completely worn away (see the wear on the stool in Plate 61).

While we no longer have the need to raise our feet above drafty floors, a foot stool can still be a comfortable adjunct to an easy chair, as well as an attractive piece of furniture in a living room or den.

CHAPTER SIX

BEDS

While rural Pennsylvania made important contributions to our heritage of bed furnishings, such as quilts, coverlets, and comforters, its corresponding contribution to the evolution of the bed itself was negligible. There is no such thing as a typical Pennsylvania bed, and any antique bed discovered in the Pennsylvania countryside would be the counterpart of many others from rural areas of contemporary states. As in any farming area, the more elaborate tester or field beds were practically nonexistent in rural Pennsylvania. It seems likely that prior to the start of the American Empire period (about 1820), many of our country ancestors slept on pallets of straw or on corn husk mattresses. Further, it seems reasonable that when simple frame beds began to appear in the hinterlands, their style, though greatly simplified, would follow the style currently popular in the cities. Thus we can explain the lack of more elaborate beds in areas remote from the furniture centers. This explanation discounts the ever-present survival examples, pieces produced by country craftsmen working from memory, without the tools, skill, or desire to reproduce the detail of the elaborate pieces they recalled.

Almost without exception, the beds of the period under consideration were designed so that the mattress was supported by a lacing of rope. It is true that some beds were equipped with a heavy piece of canvas to support the mattress, but this canvas was attached to the frame by a rope lacing. The rope was attached to the bed by one of two methods: either the rails on all four sides were pierced by evenly spaced holes through which the rope was threaded, or a series of mushroom-shaped knobs, around which the rope could be looped, were set into the tops of the rails.

Until about 1830 bed rails were morticed into the posts, and the frames were held together by the tension of the rope lacing, sometimes reinforced by long screws (bed bolts) inserted through the posts into the ends of the rails. The concealed bed catch that is used today was invented in about 1830 but did not find its way into the rural areas for a number of years.

62. Room 1141, Decorative Arts Wing, The Philadelphia Museum of Art. Note grained tester bed, half-spindle chair, decorated chest, and Mahatonga Valley chest of drawers.

Courtesy of The Philadelphia Museum of Art   *Photograph by A. J. Wyatt, Staff Photographer*

Most early beds in rural Pennsylvania were made of native woods. Maple, walnut, and cherry were the most favored for legs and posts and were also used, along with pine and poplar, for headboards, footboards, and rails. Black walnut—and woods stained to imitate it—came into favor during the Victorian period.

A word of caution is in order for those who would purchase an antique bed. It should be remembered that early beds were not built to conform to today's standard mattress sizes, so that expensive modifications, such as lengthening the side rails, are often necessary before an old bed can be adapted to modern use. An alternative is the purchase of specially built springs and mattresses to fit the old bed, but this is also expensive and can prove quite unsatisfactory, since the bed will probably still be too short for the modern man.

Tester Beds

A tester, or four poster, bed found in the countryside is either a survival example or an immigrant from one of the big cities. The one shown in Plate 62, with its simple turnings, is probably a survival type, but it is quite rare in any

104

event. This bed would make a handsome and commanding addition to a large bedroom but would be overwhelming in a small one.

Hired Man's Beds

Called a hired man's bed or an "under-the-eaves" bed, this type (see Plate 63) was popular for many years, since its small size made it well suited for use in a dormer or other small room. Both names indicate the use to which it was put.

These beds were often made without a footboard, but this was not always the case. Some were made with the headboard and footboard identical, a characteristic which, unfortunately, has led to the mutilation of many good pieces; the current vogue for twin beds (which were simply not made until this century) has resulted in the headboard and footboard of many a hired man's bed being separated to create headboards for a pair of twin beds.

63. Hired man's bed, Circa 1840   *Photograph by Charles R. Steitz, Jr.*

High-post Beds

A few high-post beds are to be found in the countryside, but they are almost invariably survival examples. The turnings are usually less elaborate than those on the example in Plate 64, and when a footboard is present it is always much lower than the headboard. The headboard is frequently not an integral part of the bed but is mounted to the insides of the posts with an arrangement of hooks and eyes so that it can be lifted out at will.

64. High-post bed, Circa 1830   *Photograph by Charles R. Steitz, Jr.*

Low-post Beds

By far the most common of the antique beds still found in rural Pennsylvania is the low-post bed as shown in Plate 65. This type differs from the high-post in the length of the posts and in the fastening of the headboard. In the low-post bed the headboard was usually morticed tightly into the posts and was not removable. Low-post rope beds were made throughout the Pennsylvania countryside until about the beginning of the twentieth century.

106

65. Low-post bed with acorn finials, Circa 1840   *Photograph by Charles R. Steitz, Jr.*

Jenny Lind Beds

The Jenny Lind, or spool, bed is an inexpensive, factory-made bed that was introduced about 1840 and is still being made. Although there are a few to be found in rural Pennsylvania, this style never seemed to gain the great popularity here that it enjoyed in other parts of the country. Since it was designed as a piece of "cottage" furniture, however, it can make an attractive addition to a Pennsylvania country bedroom.

CHAPTER SEVEN

MISCELLANEOUS

Many articles of antique furniture, particularly those of a specialized nature, cannot easily be fitted into any of the general categories discussed in the foregoing chapters. Most pieces of this type were created to answer the special needs of a society during a particular period of its sociological and technological advance. Thus, this chapter will be devoted to that furniture developed and built by our country forefathers to fill these specific requirements. We shall restrict ourselves, however, to a discussion of pieces that are readily adaptable to the needs and fancies of the present generation.

Bucket Benches

A direct outgrowth of the wash bench described in Chapter 5 is the bucket bench, an innovation probably inspired by some old-timer's difficulty in bending over. Basically just a set of shelves with the topmost shelf about 3 feet from the floor, it served to raise the wash bucket to a more comfortable height while providing additional shelves for storage below (see Plate 66). A very early arrangement, the bucket bench was built from early in the seventeenth century until late in the nineteenth. The cruder examples are simply a series of shelves (often three) nailed to uprights. The better ones are quite well constructed, with the shelves morticed into the sides and a backboard at the top of each shelf. The uppermost backboard and the front and top edges of the sides of better examples are usually slightly scrolled, and the bottom edge of each side is cut in a semicircle (or scrolled) to give the effect of feet. Usually of pine or poplar, bucket benches are also occasionally found in walnut or cherry, and these, of course, are the more desirable.

66. Bucket bench, Circa 1850. Rough, as found.

Courtesy of Mr. and Mrs. David Reed   *Photograph by Charles R. Steitz, Jr.*

Dry Sinks

By far the most popular piece of country furniture at present is the dry sink. This article, designed as a prosaic, utilitarian addition to the back porch or kitchen, has become much sought after for use in the living room, dining room, or den. These pieces are used as serving tables, china cupboards, bars, hi-fi cabinets, or a combination of any of these. Originally intended simply as a repository for the wash bucket, the dry sink is the natural result of evolution from the wash bench through the bucket bench. The first step was to add doors

67. Simple dry sink, Pine, Circa 1865
Courtesy of Dr. and Mrs. James G. Mackey   *Photograph by Charles R. Steitz, Jr.*

to enclose the lower shelves of a bucket bench, and that was followed by the logical addition of a rim, or gallery, around the top to prevent the bucket from being knocked off. Undoubtedly, the first few buckets that were accidentally tipped into the then recessed top led to the idea of providing it with a water-proof liner of copper or zinc. Most of the dry sinks seen today are so equipped. Most sinks (or zinks) date only from the late nineteenth century, but they have been collected so avidly that they are becoming relatively scarce. Even the simple ones, like the one pictured in Plate 67, are fast disappearing, so it is not surprising that the more elaborate ones (Plate 68), with a shelf built over the sink and a row of shallow drawers under the shelf, are virtually impossible to find.

Sinks of the type described above are actually transition pieces between the low sink discussed earlier and the high sink, pictured in Plate 69. The high sink, with its sink below and cupboard above, was definitely a kitchen piece. In fact, the kitchens of many homes constructed around the turn of the century

111

68. Dry sink with shelf and drawers, Circa 1850

Courtesy of Mr. and Mrs. Charles Supplee   *Photograph by Charles R. Steitz, Jr.*

were equipped with built-in sinks of this type, much as cabinets are built into kitchens today.

As is always the case with furniture originally intended to be painted, dry sinks of all three types can be found in any native wood, or any combination of native woods, pine and poplar being the most common. The hardware is almost invariably factory-made, spring catches and butt hinges predominating. The drawer pulls are usually wooden mushroom knobs, although some sinks are found with porcelain knobs or carved wooden pulls.

69. High sink, Pine, Circa 1860
Courtesy of Mr. and Mrs. C. W. Bretz   *Photograph by Charles R. Steitz, Jr.*

113

70. Small dough tray, Poplar, Circa 1870. Legs added.

Photograph by Charles R. Steitz, Jr.

Dough Troughs and Dough Trays

Two other articles of country furniture that have gained great popularity recently are the ordinary dough tray and dough trough. Basically just covered rectangular boxes with sides and ends that flare outward from the bottom, these articles have become a "must" in any scheme of country decoration. They have been used in the modern home as end tables, coffee tables, record cabinets, and receptacles for overshoes by the back door.

The chief difference between a dough tray and a dough trough is one of size. The dough tray, which was designed to be stored in the bottom of a flour bin, is considerably smaller than the dough trough, which was built on legs and equipped with an oversized top. Actually, there is very little difference in capacity between the two. The smaller one, shown in Plate 70, has a box which measures 32 by 17 by 10 inches, compared with the 37 by 16 by 12 inches of the larger (Plate 71). The illusion of size in the latter is due to the oversized top, the length of its legs, and the depth of the apron connecting the legs.

114

71. Large dough trough, Pine, Circa 1860   *Photograph by Charles R. Steitz, Jr.*

The top of the dough tray would have provided the baker with an ideal kneading board, but it was too small for the purpose. A larger top was the obvious solution, but since raw dough is quite heavy, the top tended to tip from the box when the dough was placed too close to the edge. With typical ingenuity our early craftsmen solved the problem by using deep battens on the underside of the top that were set flush with the ends of the box, and at an angle conforming to their flare (see Plate 71). This arrangement prevented the top from tipping but also made it impossible to lift the top from the box. The top could be removed by sliding it toward the front or the back until the battens completely cleared the box.

The better dough trays (and troughs) were dovetailed at the corners of the box—no mean feat, since the sides and ends were both flared outward from the bottom. The legs on the larger and better troughs were attached to the apron by mortice and tenon joints and pegged with wooden pegs, exactly as table legs and aprons were fastened together.

Although dough trays and dough troughs were occasionally treated with red filler, they seldom seem to have been painted, possibly because they were easier to keep clean if left unpainted.

As is so often the case with country furniture, pieces of this type were made throughout the entire period of our concern—and probably for many years

72. Flour bin, Pine, Circa 1870   *Photograph by Charles R. Steitz, Jr.*

later—so that age must be determined by construction details and the usual signs of age (see Chapter 9). They are usually found in pine or poplar, and if refinished naturally with just a little stain for darkening, they make a handsome addition to any country setting. A good one is well worth the search.

Flour Bins

A companion piece to the dough tray—but for some reason considerably harder to find—is the flour bin. A rather large piece of furniture (the one in Plate 72, a small one, measures 41 by 23 by 38 inches), the flour bin also was intended originally for kitchen use. It was designed to provide storage space for the family supply of flour, as well as for the dough tray during the occasional periods when it was not in use. Though the flour bin was built in one piece, it was actually divided into two separate compartments, the upper for storing the flour and the lower for storing the dough tray. The upper compartment was further divided into two sections, a small one for fine flour and a larger one for common flour. In the example in Plate 72, the capacity of the smaller section (on the left) is further reduced by the addition of a drawer at its bottom. Both flour sections are reached by lifting a single lid much like the lid of a blanket chest or wood box. (As a matter of fact, the entire upper section of a flour bin very much resembles a wood box, with the sides nailed, not dovetailed, to the ends. This type of construction indicates that the flour bin was not considered a particularly fine piece of furniture.) The lower section of a flour bin is simply a long, low storage area with space enough to house a dough tray; it is equipped with two doors which swing open from the ends.

Like so many of our old pieces, the flour bin can be adapted to various modern uses. The one in Plate 72 is being used as a bar, but like the dry sink it can be used as a serving table, hi-fi cabinet, or what have you. Perhaps its very adaptability is responsible for its scarcity, since after the advent of packaged flour, many flour bins were relegated to the barn where they lent themselves nicely as feed bins. Once they were in the barn, neglect, weather, and rats took a heavy toll.

Butcher Blocks

A piece of furniture that has come a long way up in the world is the once lowly butcher block. It has moved from the butchering shed, through the kitchen and game room, often to come to rest in the living room.

The butcher block is simply a slice cut from the trunk of a hardwood tree and mounted on legs. Depending on the thickness of the slice and the length of the legs, an old block often is used now as a coffee table, end table, or utility table. Their original owners never painted them, so the type of finish applied today is completely a matter of personal taste.

That seems to be all there is to say about butcher blocks, except that if one is found the size of the example in Plate 73, it would be wise to get help before attempting to move it.

Butcher Tables

Like the butcher block, the butcher table (Plate 74) also has come a long way. Although many are still being used for home butchering, they often appear at auctions and in country antique shops, and with a little imagination can be nicely adapted to many uses. Again, the desired use dictates the leg length. A coffee table can be achieved by shortening the legs, while a serving table or counter will require longer ones.

117

73. Butcher's block, Sycamore   *Photograph by Charles R. Steitz, Jr.*

The top of a butcher table is often a 2-inch plank of hardwood, frequently white oak, maple, or walnut, any one of which will take a beautiful finish despite the scratches and cuts that indicate its original use and enhance its antique value.

74. Butcher's table, Oak. Rough, as found.　　*Photograph by Charles R. Steitz, Jr.*

Buggy and Sleigh Seats

The buggy or sleigh seat is a piece of furniture that has only recently come into demand, and indeed has only recently come to be considered furniture. These seats were usually built as an integral part of the vehicle and should not be confused with the earlier wagon seat, which was actually a double chair placed in the back of a wagon for additional passengers. The one exception is the type shown in Plate 75, which is a removable child's seat with a back that could be folded down for convenient storage. This one has had legs added so that it can be used in the home.

Buggy seats, such as the one in Plate 76, with and without springs, are now being mounted on legs, reupholstered with foam rubber under brightly colored fabrics, and used in almost every room of today's home.

Slaw Cutters

Large slaw (or cabbage) cutters, which a few years ago were almost impossible for a dealer to sell, now also are being set on legs and used as coffee tables or end tables (see Plate 77). Usually of oak or some other hardwood, they take a nice finish and can look quite attractive in an informal setting. The sliding box on the top of the cutter is usually of pine and can be fitted with a bottom, lined with copper, and used as a planter.

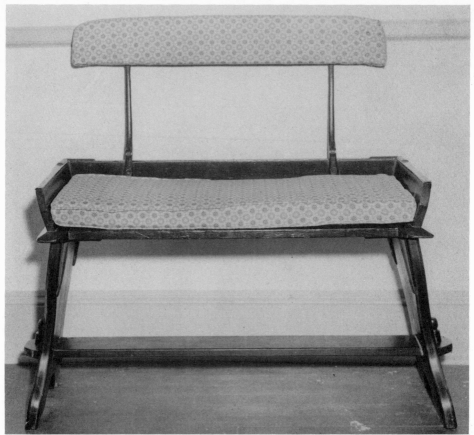

75. Child's buggy seat   *Photograph by Charles R. Steitz, Jr.*

76. Buggy seat   *Photograph by Charles R. Steitz, Jr.*

120

77. Large slaw cutter. Legs added.

Courtesy of Dr. and Mrs. James G. Mackey   *Photograph by Charles R. Steitz, Jr.*

Cradles

Cradles, which are always in demand, can be as simple as the one in Plate 78 or as elaborate as that in Plate 79. The simple ones are found with or without hoods and with solid, rope, or slat bottoms. Those made by the Pennsylvania Dutch were usually decorated, sometimes quite lavishly. In addition to the usual painted or stencilled decoration, they frequently have pierced designs, such as heart-shaped handles, at the head and foot. Excessive wear is sometimes found on the tops of the runner ends, one effect of many generations of mothers who rocked the baby with their feet while keeping their hands busy at other tasks.

Spool Cabinets

A piece of equipment from the old country store that has gained great popularity is the spool cabinet (see Plate 80). Found with two, three, or four drawers, they are used to good advantage as silver chests or trinket boxes. Since they were often made of walnut, cherry, or pine, any of which takes superlative finish, they can be quite attractive in the proper setting.

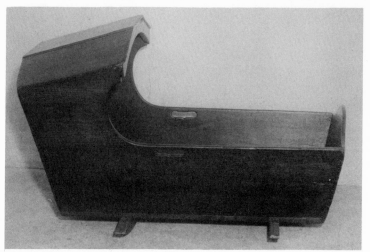

78. Hooded cradle, Walnut, Circa 1800

Courtesy of Mr. and Mrs. Robert Levison　　　　　　*Photograph by Charles R. Steitz, Jr.*

79. Spool-turned cradle, Circa 1860. Rough, as found.

Photograph by Charles R. Steitz, Jr.

80. Spool cabinet, Walnut, Circa 1880

Courtesy of Mr. and Mrs. T. A. Rosensteel　　　　　　*Photograph by Charles R. Steitz, Jr.*

81. Spinning wheel
Courtesy of Mr. and Mrs. Charles Supplee   *Photograph by Charles R. Steitz, Jr.*

Spinning Wheels, Wool Wheels, and Cobbler's Benches

Articles of this nature were tools, designed for specific purposes, and have absolutely no useful function in any but the most unusual of today's homes. They do, however, serve as good "props" and, used with discrimination, can aid materially in establishing a country antique tone in a room (see Plates 81, 82 and 83).

82. Wool wheel

Courtesy of Mr. and Mrs. Elmer Meng, Jr.　　　　　　　*Photograph by Charles R. Steitz, Jr.*

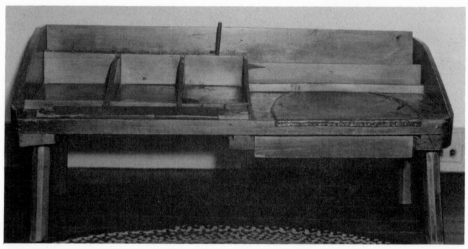

83. Cobbler's bench

Courtesy of Mr. and Mrs. Robert C. Dewey　　　　　　　*Photograph by Charles R. Steitz, Jr.*

124

CHAPTER EIGHT

TREENWARE

It must be remembered that our rural ancestors, unlike many of their urban contemporaries, usually had little or no money to spare. This is not to suggest that they all were poor, because many were quite well-to-do, having extensive fields, plenty of livestock, substantial homes, and large, well-fed families. They were short of actual currency, however, simply because there was not a large supply of it available in the countryside. This lack of a medium of exchange forced the residents into an economic system largely based on barter and taught them to become expert at improvising articles they could not afford to buy. Although iron, tin, pewter, and china were in common use in seaports, where money was plentiful, wooden (treenware) articles had to serve in the interior. There we can still find bowls, spoons, paddles, measures, and a host of other articles all made of wood, while pieces of this sort seldom turn up in the cities. Although none of these can properly be classified as furniture, they were so much a part of country living, and are now so important to country decorative schemes, that we feel justified in including them in this book.

Kitchen Implements and Tools

A bread board, such as the one shown in Plate 84, was put to many uses by the country housewife. It was used as a flat surface on which to roll dough for cookies and pie crusts and as a cutting board on which to slice bread, cut cookies, and chop vegetables. Many of these chores are still faced by the modern housewife, so bread boards remain popular items. They can be found in a variety of shapes, frequently with the hole by which they were hung on the wall cut into a decorative pattern. Although popular, bread boards are relatively plentiful, and good ones can still be acquired at a reasonable 'price.

Slaw cutters much smaller than those mentioned in the preceding chapter were almost indispensable, at least as far as the Pennsylvania Dutch housewife was concerned. Without a slaw cutter there would have been no sauerkraut or cole slaw, and mama would have had a most unhappy family. Although few women today make their own sauerkraut, a slaw cutter can still be quite handy when it comes to cutting cabbage for cole slaw or slicing potatoes thin enough for the best frying. They were made in many sizes and shapes and with or without adjustable blades, and the later ones are still plentiful.

Wooden bowls are found in a great variety of sizes and shapes, but the most attractive of all are those that were cut from the burl of a hardwood tree. (A burl is the large growth or protuberance often seen growing on the side of a walnut or other hardwood tree.) The random pattern of graining in a burl produces a bowl that is not only beautiful, but also unlikely to split as a result of shrinking. It has been said that the Indians taught the colonists the art of making bowls from a burl.

Unfortunately, burl bowls are quite rare today, and when one comes on the market, it is usually sold at a premium price. This is not to say that wooden bowls in general are hard to find. Bowls such as the example in Plate 84, which were cut from the trunk of a tree rather than from a burl, are relatively common and are used in many modern households for serving salads, fruit, or nuts. Some are also used as knitting bowls, in which case they are usually mounted on legs to raise them to a more convenient height.

The production of apple butter, so dear to the hearts of the Pennsylvania Dutch, has given us the broad, long-handled stirrers and paddles shown in Plate 84. The stirrers, which functioned better with a hole in their working end, are a rich field for studying the Dutch art of pierced decoration. These stirrers and paddles are rather easily found but serve no useful purpose today, other than as decorative accessories.

The pestle-shaped implements shown in Plate 84 apparently had many uses in the kitchens of yesteryear. As nearly as we can determine, the smaller ones were used in conjunction with a funnel-shaped tin arrangement to stuff meat into sausages, while the larger ones were used in the production of sauerkraut.

The art (or science) of butter-making has given today's collector an extensive and completely separate field of interest. We are referring, of course, to the collecting of butter molds. Usually made by machine, these molds can be found in a surprising number of sizes, shapes, and patterns. They range in size from the individual pat molds to the full pound size (Plate 85) and can be found in round, square, or rectangular shapes. Real variety is found, however, in the patterns which were carved into the face of the mold to allow a design to be

84. Kitchen implements. Bread board, small slaw cutters, wooden bowl, stuffers, and apple butter stirrer.   *Photograph by Charles R. Steitz, Jr.*

85. Butter molds
Courtesy of Dr. and Mrs. Laverne J. Junker   *Photograph by Charles R. Steitz, Jr.*

86. Wooden pitchfork and rake
Courtesy of Mr. and Mrs. T. A. Rosensteel   *Photograph by Charles R. Steitz, Jr.*

impressed on the finished butter. Among the host of different patterns are eagles, sheaves of wheat, and, most appropriately, cows. They are all avidly collected, but so many were made that not all have as yet found their way into collections. They still appear rather frequently at sales and in antique shops and can usually be purchased at reasonable prices. Other butter-making tools are the butter scoop (used for filling the mold), the churn, and the butter tub (or firkin), none of which, however, are as fascinating to the collector as the butter mold.

Wooden spoons have, of course, been with us for a long, long time. There is really very little to be said about them, except that old ones are seldom found, largely because of the hard daily use to which they were subjected.

Wooden tools, for both indoor and outdoor work, were as essential to our forefathers as wooden kitchen utensils were to their wives. The pitchfork and rake shown in Plate 86 are two of the most common outdoor tools. They were factory-produced in great numbers and are still fairly easy to find.

128

87. Molding planes, jack planes, and block plane

Photograph by Charles R. Steitz, Jr.

In the days before the combination plane and the mechanical shaper, a cabinetmaker had to own, in addition to his jack and block planes, a complete set of molding planes (see Plate 87). He had to have one for each shape that he produced, so the number of planes owned by one man sometimes ran into the dozens. Even though they were factory-made, all wooden planes, particularly molding planes, are avidly collected today, some to be used in reproducing the old shapes and some merely for props.

Wooden containers were produced in great numbers and in many different styles and are still relatively easy to find. Metal-banded tubs, buckets, and grain measures (Plate 88) are the most common, although double measures (which measured a different quantity from each end) are becoming somewhat scarce. Keelers (maple sugar buckets), while still available in the sugaring country of western Pennsylvania, are rapidly disappearing as the growers replace them with plastic bags or with miles of plastic tubing. That so many keelers have survived the ravages of time and weather is mute testimony to the excellence of their construction. Made entirely by hand and as individual as fingerprints, they are held together by wooden bands which expand and contract along with the staves as the keeler absorbs or gives up moisture. This characteristic has kept many of them tight and serviceable for years and makes them ideal as outdoor wastebaskets or, when filled with sand, as patio ashtrays. They have also gained great popularity in recent years as magazine holders and wastebaskets in informal settings within the home.

88. Wooden measures and keelers   *Photograph by Charles R. Steitz, Jr.*

89. Beehive baskets   *Photograph by Charles R. Steitz, Jr.*

130

90. Bootjack, footwarmer, bellows, and coffee grinder

Photograph by Charles R. Steitz, Jr.

Although not properly classified as treenware, we feel that the inclusion of woven, or "beehive," baskets at this point would not be too far amiss. These practical and attractive baskets are becoming somewhat hard to find because of their perishable nature, so the acquisition of one in reasonably good condition can be considered a stroke of luck. They were made in a great many sizes and shapes for an equally large number of uses, and the utilization of a particular basket today depends on its size and shape. Plate 89 shows two sizes, the smaller of which suggests use as a fruit bowl, while the larger might be employed as a magazine holder.

Articles such as bellows and coffee grinders require little explanation. Suffice it to say that while items of this nature are still functional accessories in the modern home, none of them of any age at all are very easy to come by. Other articles such as foot warmers (with tin liners) and boot jacks (see Plate 90) turn up occasionally, but they have outlived their usefulness and must be classified as decorative props.

Clothes hangers, surprisingly enough, are not a recent invention. Simple ones, fashioned from a barrel stave or simply a bent branch, have been around for many years. They were suspended by a piece of twine or a leather thong, tied around the exact center of the hanger, and can still be used to hang clothes from pegs or hooks, just as their makers intended.

CHAPTER NINE

SIGNS OF AGE

It has been mentioned several times that the survival nature of country furniture renders accurate dating based on style alone quite difficult. Taking this one step further, we can say that just as survival examples exist with respect to style, so do they exist with respect to features of workmanship and construction. Methods of workmanship and details of construction were often continued in remote areas long after they were practically forgotten in the population centers. Therefore, dates mentioned in the following sections are applicable to country furniture, not to furniture produced in the manufacturing and style centers. (Figure 17 in the back section of this book summarizes the signs of age discussed in this and the following chapter.)

Patina

This elusive word is bandied about quite freely by antique enthusiasts, both expert and novice, frequently without any accurate notion of its meaning, to say nothing of its pronunciation. Webster defines "patina" as "a green film formed on copper and bronze by oxidation, and esteemed in art," and later as "a surface mellowing and softening, as in color, with age or use." When an antique collector mentions patina, he is using it in the latter sense to describe the color or "complexion" which wood acquires with age. All wood will darken to some degree when exposed to the air over a long period of time, and in this oxidation lies the connection between Webster's first and second definitions. Pine, for example, goes from its very light color when freshly cut through all shades of brown, becoming almost black after two hundred-odd years of exposure to air. If different parts of an old piece have had different degrees of exposure, they will be of noticeably different shades of brown, even though they are all of the same wood. Thus, the inside of the back of a bureau desk, for example, will be lighter than the outside of the back, and the insides of all the drawers will be an altogether different shade. All corresponding sections, however, such as the drawer bottoms, will be of the same shade.

Unfortunately, there is no gauge as to how much darkening should take place in a given type of wood over a given number of years. Not only do the various woods react differently to exposure to air, but also there is nothing standard about the reaction of different samples of the same wood. All this means that while patina is certainly a *guide* to age, it does not indicate any specific date. It can be used effectively to spot restorations and to some extent to judge *relative* age, but it cannot be used to pinpoint, or even to bracket, a date with any degree of certainty. Patina is the sort of tool that grows more valuable with the collector's experience. As one gets the "feel" for the proper patina under certain conditions of age and exposure to air, one can become more sure of his judgment of relative age based on the appearance of the patina.

There is a myth currently in wide circulation that when many layers of paint are removed from the surface of an old piece, the worker will expose the old wood, complete with the delightful patina that comes with age. Anyone who has ever removed paint spots or rings from the top of an old table knows that this certainly is not true. Occasionally, for example, old tables with the paint long since worn off (or ones that were never painted) are relegated to service in the workshop, where they acquire various splashes and rings of new paint. When these spots are removed (carefully, with a good remover and no scraping), the areas which were covered by the new paint are invariably lighter in color than the rest of the surface. If there is any patina present, it was there before the new paint was acquired or is the result of the action on the wood of the solvent in the paint.

Tool Marks

Since the early cabinetmaker worked with many tools no longer used in modern furniture factories, it stands to reason that those tools left marks not found on new furniture. The first mark that we will consider, however, is a tool mark that was left on the wood before it was ready for the cabinetmaker's bench. When boards are rough-sawn from the raw logs, there is always a distinct and clearly visible mark left along the length of the board by the saw that did the work. Since over the years there have been several radical changes in the design of these saws, we are able, by examining the saw mark, to determine with reasonable accuracy the period of history during which a particular board was ripped from its log.

The earliest boards produced in this country were hand-ripped by a team of two men using an arrangement known as a pit saw. In this operation the log was suspended above a pit or elevated on a pair of trestles, and the two men, one above and one below, pulled a single saw vertically through the length of the log. This alternate pulling from above and below left marks on the plank that, while straight, were always at some angle to the grain and never parallel to one another. Although the presence of pit-saw marks on a piece of furniture—the back of a cupboard, for instance—is a good indication that the piece is quite old, we cannot use these marks to establish any precise date, because lumber was still being sawn in the pits long after the gash saw came into general use.

The gash saw was similar to the pit saw in that it had straight blades which moved vertically through the log. It differed in that it was mechanically operated (usually water-powered) and had several parallel blades, which permitted the sawing of several boards simultaneously. This type of saw also left straight marks on the wood, but these were always perpendicular to the grain and parallel to one another. Again, it is not wise to attempt to date a piece by the presence of gash-saw marks, since the use of this saw overlapped the use of the pit saw and was, in turn, overlapped by the use of the circular saw.

The circular saw came into widespread use about 1850 and has been used almost exclusively ever since, thus finally giving us a saw mark that we can use to establish maximum age. We can safely say that if there are arc-shaped marks that seem to be concentric along the length of the board, the board was sawn from the log after 1850.

After receiving his rough-sawn lumber from the mill, the early cabinetmaker was faced with the job of smoothing it. He started with his large jack plane, the slightly convex edge of which left a series of ridges and valleys along the length of the board. If the board was to be visible in the finished piece, he usually completed the smoothing with a smaller plane; if not, he left the ridges and valleys just as they were. These marks can be found in such places as the undersides of drawers and shelves and the back surfaces of case pieces; often it is easier to feel them than to see them. Although plane marks are considered good indicators of age, the only specific thing that can be said is that they are seldom found on furniture made after 1875, when the development of mechanical milling equipment made inexpensive milled lumber available in all but the most remote areas.

Another indicator of age, though not so much a mark as an irregularity, resulted from the use of the early molding planes. The cabinetmaker was usually well equipped with a large variety of these planes, each with its edge ground to produce a particular shape. The fact that these tools were hand-operated meant that the results they produced would be something less than perfect. Consequently, measurements taken with calipers will show variances along the length of the mold such as never appear on jobs produced by modern wood-working machinery.

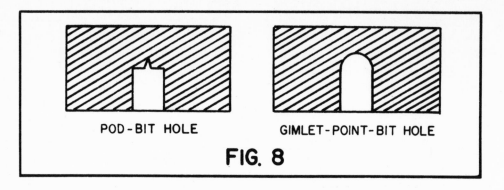

POD-BIT HOLE   GIMLET-POINT-BIT HOLE

FIG. 8

A tool mark not as readily visible as those we have just discussed is the mark left in a drilled hole by an early auger known as a pod bit. When this bit was used for a hole designed not to go all the way through the wood, it left the hole with a bowl-shaped bottom (see Figure 8). The pod bit was used until the introduction of the gimlet-point bit, which came into general use about 1850. It can be seen from Figure 8 that the gimlet-point bit left a flat-bottomed hole with the mark of the gimlet in its center.

The mark of the pod bit can be found in the socket holes of chairs made before 1850. On turned members of chairs, such as legs and posts, the positions of the sockets, as well as the positions of mortices cut to receive slats, were frequently marked by score marks. These marks were cut by the turner while the part was still in the lathe and therefore run completely around the part (see Plate 91). Since score marks are never found on modern, factory-made furniture, they too are considered to be signs of age. They are not usually found on furniture made after about 1880.

Carpenters and cabinetmakers have traditionally used a scribe rather than a pencil to scratch guidelines on wood. The early cabinetmakers used the scribe to mark the intended positions of mortices or hinges on the surface of the wood or to indicate the depth to which dovetails should be cut (see Figure 9). These scribe marks are found in places not ordinarily visible and should not be confused with the score marks mentioned above. Because there is no need for these marks on machine-made furniture, scribe marks, too, never appear on furniture made after about 1880.

Dovetails

The dovetail is another dating clue widely used by collectors, expert and novice alike. It was the method most favored by early cabinetmakers when strength was the prime consideration in the angle joining of two pieces of wood. Our country craftsmen used the dovetail to join the corners of a chest or dough

91. The score marks on ladder-back chair in Plate 48

Photograph by Charles R. Steitz, Jr.

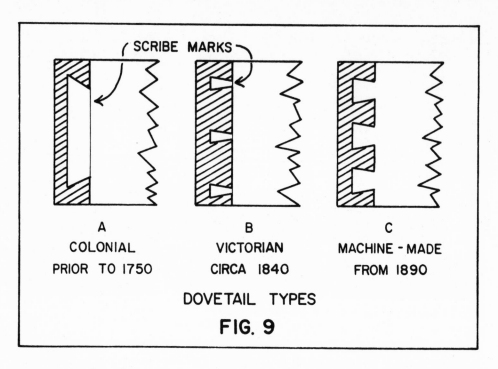

SCRIBE MARKS

A	B	C
COLONIAL	VICTORIAN	MACHINE - MADE
PRIOR TO 1750	CIRCA 1840	FROM 1890

DOVETAIL TYPES

FIG. 9

tray, to join the sides to the top and bottom of a cupboard or chest of drawers, or the sides to the front and back of a drawer. It is in the last-mentioned use that the dovetail varied most with time, so we will direct our attention to drawer construction.

It is said as a rather general rule of thumb that the larger the hand-cut dovetail, the earlier the piece, and although there are exceptions to this rule, as there are to most, it can be considered a fairly reliable one. (Note: When we speak of the *size* of a dovetail in a drawer, we refer to that portion of the joint that is an integral part of the drawer's side, as opposed to the end grain which is visible in the joint and belongs to the drawer's front or back. In Figure 9 the front of the drawer is shaded and the side is not.)

The earliest dovetailed drawers in this country were constructed with one large dovetail, almost as wide as the depth of the drawer side (see Figure 9A). This construction was gradually modified over the years as craftsmen built drawers with more and more dovetails, placed closer and closer together, until the advent of the machine-made dovetail in the last quarter of the nineteenth century. The dovetail machine is still in general use in our furniture factories, and drawers made with it today look just as they did in 1890. This machine-made dovetailing (see Figure 9C) is quite easy to identify by its uniformity and regular spacing—each dovetail is exactly like the next, and all are the same distance apart. The scribe mark, mentioned in the preceding section, is never

138

92. Dovetails in the top of a jelly cupboard   *Photograph by Charles R. Steitz, Jr.*

found on machine-made dovetailing. (See examples of dovetails of various ages in Plates 92, 93, 94 and 95.) It is a rather sad commentary on our times that with the quantity of material written on this subject, all an auctioneer has to do to get a higher price on some late Victorian monstrosity is to announce that it is "dovetailed throughout," and some eager, uninformed buyer will raise his bid.

93. Dovetails, Circa 1825   *Photograph by Charles R. Steitz, Jr.*

139

94. Dovetails, Circa 1860   *Photograph by Charles R. Steitz, Jr.*

The style of drawer front construction (with the exception of dovetail size) is of little help to us in trying to estimate the age of a country-made piece, since the country craftsman built his drawer fronts as he pleased—flush, lipped, or beaded—without regard to style or convention.

Shrinkage

All wood will shrink when it dries. This fact is equally as applicable to the kiln-dried lumber of today as it was to the earlier air-dried lumber, and shrinkage is the reason for the cracks and splits that occur in modern furniture just as it is the reason for the same kinds of cracks and splits we find in antiques. To make matters worse, there is no guarantee that wood, once dried out, will stay dry. Any wood exposed to dampness will absorb moisture and swell, and if it is then moved to a heated place, it will give up this moisture and shrink. This is why some chairs, good and tight in the summer, become loose and wobbly in the winter.

95. Machine-made dovetails   *Photograph by Charles R. Steitz, Jr.*

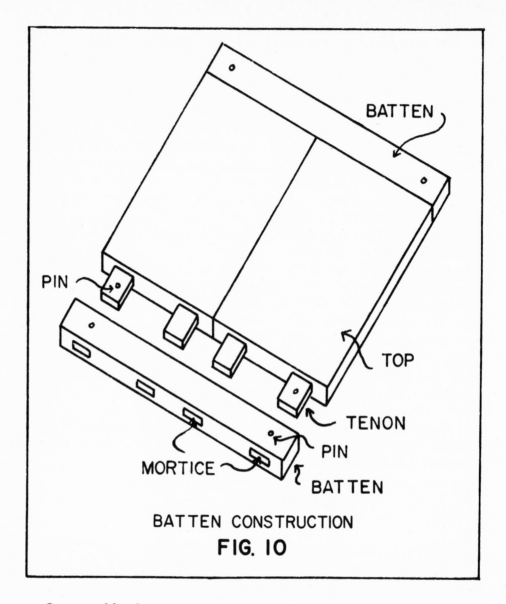

BATTEN

PIN

TOP

TENON

PIN

MORTICE

BATTEN

BATTEN CONSTRUCTION

FIG. 10

Once wood has lost its original moisture, it will never again absorb enough moisture from the air to return to its original dimensions. And since this shrinking and swelling occur across the grain of the wood, with little or no change in dimension in the direction of the grain, we have another criterion for judging the age of a piece. The round top of an old tripod stand made from a single plank will always be slightly elliptical, measuring somewhat less across the grain than with it. Similarly, old turnings also will be slightly elliptical, and although this will not be discernible to the naked eye, it will become quite apparent if the

142

turning is measured all around with a caliper. Thus, the caliper can be used to check the authenticity of a suspected turning, since a part turned from modern, kiln-dried lumber will exhibit little or no shrinking across as short a dimension as the diameter of a leg. Incidentally, this shrinking of wood was well known to our ancestors and used to good advantage by early chairmakers in constructing turned chairs. They turned legs from green lumber, which subsequently shrank and seized the rungs in a grip which in many chairs is still holding fast today.

Our early craftsmen were also aware of the damage shrinkage could cause in a flat board, and they often used batten construction, the method shown in Figure 10, to prevent this. Figure 10 is a representation of the top of a blanket chest or table in which the boards are joined by a cleat, or batten, across their ends. Each board is loosely morticed through the cleat at two places, but pinned through only one mortice, which is the secret of the success of the method (see also Plate 96). This method allows complete movement of each board throughout its width so that it can expand and contract without splitting, and at the same time it prevents the top from warping out of shape.

The results of shrinkage can often be seen on case pieces that contain stile and rail construction. The panels, which were set loosely into grooves in the edges of the stiles and rails, can be seen to have shrunk to such an extent that they have become completely separated from one or both of the stiles. This condition is most often encountered on the doors of cupboards and on the sides of chests of drawers, where wide, one-piece panels have been used.

It should be noted that shrinkage, while indicative of age, is not particularly specific. About all that we can say is that a piece with no discernible shrinkage in any of the locations just discussed was probably made after about 1910, when kiln-drying of lumber came into general use.

Wooden Pins

Wooden pins, or pegs, were used in the construction of country furniture as late as 1850, nearly one hundred years after development of a satisfactory glue rendered them obsolete in city-made furniture. They are found securing the legs to the aprons of tavern tables, farm tables, and large dough troughs and also in the stile and rail joints of cupboard and wardrobe doors. The pins were always made of a wood harder than the wood of the joint which they secured. They were never round but were intentionally left irregular so that the shoulders or edges of the pin would bite into the wood of the joint and provide additional strength.

Pins will sometimes be found protruding somewhat from one face of a table leg (see Plate 97), while those in the adjoining face remain flush with the surface. This is not because they have started to work loose, but because the

96. One mortice and tenon joint and its pin. This is the top of chest shown in Plate 18, in which the molding is used as a batten.

Photograph by Charles R. Steitz, Jr.

wood of the leg has shrunk; and since the shrinkage is only across the grain, the pins which were driven through the leg *with* the grain would not be expected to protrude.

There is a theory of joinery called the "draw bore" theory, which has given rise to a good deal of discussion. Those who espouse this theory believe that the old cabinetmakers drilled the hole in a tenon just a little off center from the corresponding hole in the mortice, so that when a pin was driven through the two holes, the joint was drawn tighter. We have removed enough kinked pins from joints that are still good and tight to believe that the proponents of this theory are probably right. Unfortunately, however, it must remain only a theory, because once a pin has been driven into a joint, the holes are forced to line up, so that even after a joint is taken apart, we cannot tell how the holes were originally positioned.

144

97. One corner of small tavern table in Plate 6. Note the wooden pins.

Photograph by Charles R. Steitz, Jr.

145

Paint

Paint on a piece of furniture can be a rather good indicator of age, but like shrinkage, it is not very precise. A glance at the spot where the leg enters the seat on the underside of a plank-bottom chair will often give a chronological record of the colors the chair has worn. People are seldom particularly careful at this point, so spots of the original paint can usually be found, overlaid by patches of each subsequent color applied.

New paint—that is, paint up to fifteen or twenty years old—comes off quite easily with paint remover, but each older layer uncovered is increasingly hard to remove. In attempting to judge the age of paint, it should be remembered that old paint will flake and chip when scraped, while newer paint will peel. Also, a sharp blow will cause old paint to shatter, much like glass, while a similar blow will simply dent new paint.

If a piece was originally painted with one of the old milk-based paints, that coat will be almost impossible to remove with anything short of lye or ammonia. (Caution: Before attempting to work with lye, refer to *The Furniture Doctor* or *From Gunk to Glow,* both by George Grotz.) If a piece was originally treated with the old red filler, as so much early country furniture was, one of the bleaching techniques must be used (again we recommend Grotz). Needless to say, if any decoration appears to have been part of the original finish, every effort should be made to preserve it, thus enhancing the value of the piece.

Glass

Old glass panes and undisturbed putty in a cupboard door can be indisputable signs of age. Glass made by the old methods usually has wavy lines and bubbles in it, and sometimes there are even ripples on its surface. Once seen, it is unmistakable. While it would be most unusual to find a cupboard with all of its old panes intact, the presence of even one original pane would go a long way toward establishing the date of the piece. Blown, or "crown," glass was used for panes until about 1850, when clearer, smoother plate glass became available.

Wear

This is perhaps the most obvious, but certainly the least definitive sign of age we will discuss. Like most other signs of age, wear can give us a great deal of general information but nothing that will enable us to pinpoint specific dates. Normal wear on a piece of furniture usually takes a considerable amount of time before it becomes severe enough to indicate great age. But wear, of course, is not always normal. If a chair, for example, is dragged around a concrete patio for a few summers, it will exhibit wear that several generations of normal use would not produce. We can train ourselves to recognize abnormal wear and refuse to buy a piece that shows it. Normal wear can be an excellent guidepost in judging the age, as well as the authenticity, of much of the antique furniture we examine.

A chair will almost always show some rounding at the bottom of its legs, since the easiest way to move a chair has always been to drag it across the floor. A chair that has been repeatedly grasped from the front and dragged from place to place will always show wear on the front edge of the front legs, never on the back edge. The back edge of the back legs may be rounded from the chair's having been dragged backwards—and from its having been tipped back by many generations of sitters. The tipping also may have contributed to a flattening of the back edge of the chair's highest points—the finials on a ladder-back, the center of the hoop on a hoop-back, or the back of the ears on a mule-ear—since these are the points which hit the wall when the chair was tipped. The rungs of chairs also receive a great deal of wear from the many people, particularly children, who like to hook their heels on the rungs while they sit. This treatment over a generation or two often results in heavy wear, usually to the top of the front rung. While the wear on the front rung will always be greatest on either side of the center, the wear on side rungs will be much greater at the front ends of the rungs, for obvious reasons. If a chair has double front rungs, the wear will be greatest on the bottom rung, unless it is a child's chair.

The ends of the softwood arms of chairs, such as those on the firehouse Windsor (or captain's chair) shown in Plate 53, often show considerable wear from the unintentional polishing by many hands.

Rocking chairs present a slightly different picture. The most obvious place to look for wear on rockers is the bottom of the runners. Unlike other chairs, the wear on the front rung of a rocker is liable to be on the bottom, rather than on the top. This is because the rung of a rocker was not so comfortable for the sitter to hang his heels from, but it did rub against his leg as he rocked back and forth. Wear of this nature is usually very slight and frequently can be felt more readily than seen.

Edges and corners of exposed areas on antique furniture are invariably found to have been blunted or gently rounded by normal wear. They remain sharp and new-looking only in areas where they have been completely protected from contact with other objects, including the human body. The tops of old tables and chests, for example, will never be found with sharp edges or corners.

The bottom edge of a drawer side is one area in which normal wear can always be found. Because of the downward tilt of a partially opened drawer,

98. Normal wear on a cupboard door caused by blade of the latch striking door frame

Photograph by Charles R. Steitz, Jr.

the edge will be worn in a gentle curve, deeper toward the front of the drawer than toward the back. The drawer slide (upon which the bottom edge of the drawer runs) will show corresponding wear, usually in the form of a groove slightly wider than the drawer side.

It should also be noted that normal wear can be seen on a door where for a period of time the blade of the latch has often struck the frame (see Plate 98).

Of course, anything that people would have habitually grasped—such as a drawer pull, a door pull, or a door edge—will show wear and polishing, and a large amount of such wear is an excellent sign of age.

148

99. Bottom of one of the chairs in Plate 49 showing branded mark of Wm. Lee

Photograph by Charles R. Steitz, Jr.

Signed Furniture

The presence of a craftsman's signature on a piece of furniture is the most definitive sign of age we can find—provided, of course, that the maker's signature and period of work have been recorded. While it is still possible to find furniture in the Pennsylvania hinterlands made by recognized craftsmen (such as the chair in Plate 49), the majority of signed pieces, such as that in Plate 100, are the work of unrecorded craftsmen. Although much work has gone into recording the makers of formal or "important" furniture, there is a vast amount of research yet to be done in the field of country furniture. It is hoped that Mrs. Shiffer's recently published and excellent book *Furniture and Its Makers of Chester County, Pennsylvania* will spark others to this type of exhaustive research in their own areas.

149

100. Branded mark of W. C. Sickler on bottom of a plank-bottom chair. Maker unrecorded. *Photograph by Charles R. Steitz, Jr.*

Signed furniture can help us to date a piece in still another way, since it is sometimes possible to attribute an unsigned piece to a specific maker by comparing it with his known work. If a recorded maker is known, for example, to favor some particular methods of construction or detail that also appear on an unsigned piece, it is often safe to attribute the unsigned example to him. A word of caution, however: comparison of this nature is a highly specialized field which requires a great deal of time and study before one is well enough acquainted with any particular type of furniture to be able to attribute an unsigned piece to a specific maker.

150

CHAPTER TEN

HARDWARE

As mentioned previously, hardware can be a great aid in establishing the production date of antique furniture. Extreme care must be taken, however, to be sure that the hardware is original. Hinges and drawer pulls were susceptible to injury; pulls were changed to meet the whims of style; screws worked loose and required replacement, and latch springs wore out and broke—to mention just a few of the honest reasons why a piece may be found with hardware that is not original. Unfortunately, there are other reasons, and not all of them are honest. A country chest of drawers, for instance, might be more desirable if Chippendale brasses were substituted for its original wooden knobs, or "H" hinges replacing the original butt hinges might make a simple corner cupboard more attractive. It is regrettable that the excellent reproduction hardware so often necessary in authentic restoration is also available to the antique faker. This hardware, which is often a close enough copy to deceive all but the most discriminating observer, is manufactured in good faith by a few reputable firms to fill the needs of equally reputable manufacturers of reproduction furniture. Its availability is also a boon to the restorer of antique furniture, since even the purist must occasionally be satisfied with good reproduction hardware to replace missing or broken parts. This practice is perfectly acceptable as long as the reproduction hardware is called to the attention of the prospective buyer, but since there are still a few sellers who believe in the old admonition *caveat emptor*, we who would buy wisely must learn to distinguish the old from the new. Fortunately, old hardware has characteristics that are seldom incorporated into later examples, and it is the purpose of this chapter to familiarize the reader with some of these characteristics.

151

Nails

The lowly nail is the one type of old hardware that has never been debased by misguided attempts at reproduction. This fact, coupled with their relative scarcity, tends to make early nails an important guidepost in establishing authenticity.

Nails were used in the production of furniture throughout the period we are studying, and the intended use of the nails usually dictated their shape. Early hinges were often attached by large-headed, hand-forged nails that were driven completely through the wood and clinched (see Plates 103 and 104). Finishing nails, on the other hand, were meant to be as inconspicuous as possible and consequently were made with very small heads or with no heads at all. Between these two types can be found an entire range of hand-forged nails, with varying sizes of heads and shanks, each one suited for a specific purpose. No two of these old nails are ever exactly alike, since each was made separately and by hand, but they will invariably be found with a square shank and usually —but not always—a sharp point. Early nails were made of a fine but soft grade of Russian or Swedish iron. This was a strong material that was further strengthened by the compacting inherent in hand forging. The nails produced were not only strong, but also quite ductile, which made them ideal for situations that required them to be clinched.

The hand-forged nail, in its several forms, was made until the invention of the cut nail machine in about 1790. As with everything else, however, the practice of using hand-forged nails lasted longer in rural than in urban areas, so 1800–1810 is probably the better cutoff date for our purposes. Plate 101 shows a group of the more common hand-forged nails.

Cut nails are characterized chiefly by their similarity to one another. Every nail of the same type produced on the same machine looks exactly like every other one. They were usually made with blunt points and near the head were always rectangular in cross section. Since these nails were cut from sheet metal, one dimension (the thickness of the sheet) had to remain constant; thus any tapering had to be on the remaining two sides. Consequently, the cross section varies from the definite rectangle near the head to a square as the shank tapers toward the point. Slight ridges, left by the cutting machine, usually can be found on the tapered edges. Like forged nails, cut nails were produced in many sizes and shapes, each designed for a specific purpose. Since they are roughly contemporary with machine-made screws (which replaced nails for attaching hinges), cut nails with large heads were not produced in any quantity. A variety of cut nails is also shown in Plate 101.

Since these nails are still being produced, we can safely say that a piece of furniture in which only cut nails were used was made some time after 1800.

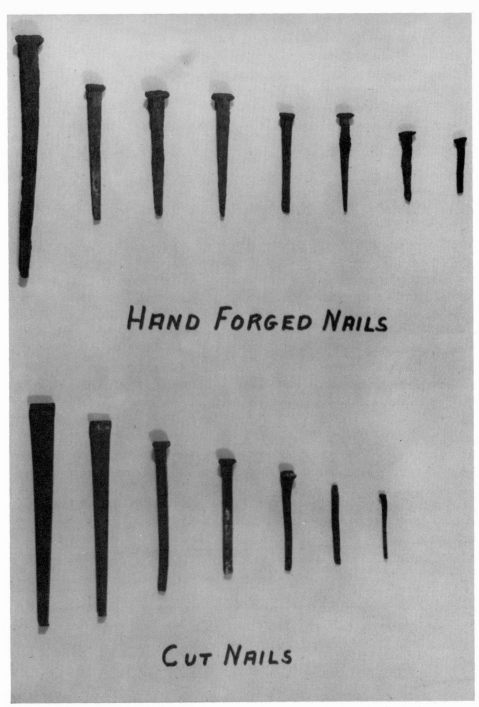

HAND FORGED NAILS

CUT NAILS

101. Hand-forged and cut nails   *Photograph by Charles R. Steitz, Jr.*

We occasionally come across a piece that has been repaired with cut nails but obviously predates 1800. In such a case there will always be some evidence of older methods of construction.

Because of the scarcity of upholstered pieces, old tacks are rather uncommon in country furniture, so we will mention them only in passing. All that really need be said is that the general appearance of tacks has changed very little over the years; a tack produced today looks much like a tack made in 1820.

Screws

Another fastener that has been with us a long time is the wood screw. Screws were used in furniture as far back as the beginning of the eighteenth century, and like nails, the early ones were hand-forged. These hand-forged screws were made simply by cutting threads on a rounded shank, and the results were quite crude. The threads were uneven, the heads irregular, and the slot for the screwdriver narrow, shallow, and usually off center. The ends of these early screws did not come to a point, but were cut off square, thus making it necessary for a hole to be drilled before the screw was started into the wood. Hand-forged screws were used for such jobs as fastening tabletops to their aprons (from the bottom), attaching drop-leaf table hinges, and occasionally fastening ornamental cupboard hinges.

The early nineteenth century saw the invention of several screw-cutting machines, which were able to produce screws so inexpensively that hand-forged screws were almost immediately priced out of the market, even in the most remote areas. While machine-made screws had more regular shanks and threads than their predecessors, they continued to have blunt ends and irregular heads with narrow, off-center slots. It wasn't until about 1860 that the modern gimlet-point wood screw replaced the earlier ones.

While the presence of modern screws in a piece of furniture does not necessarily prove lack of age, the presence of early screws can be an excellent indicator of antiquity, especially if there is no evidence of tampering.

Hinges

One of the earliest metal hinges used on furniture in this country was the cotter pin hinge, or staple hinge (see Plate 102). It was quite simple in construction, consisting of two iron cotter pins looped together. They were attached to the piece by thrusting one of the pins through a hole drilled diagonally through the stationary member of the joint, and the other through a similar hole in the movable member. The ends of the pins, protruding through the holes, were then clinched (bent flat) and driven back into the wood, much like a staple. Since

154

102. Cotter pin (or staple) hinge   *Photograph by Charles R. Steitz, Jr.*

these hinges were weak and not capable of resisting much punishment, they frequently worked loose or broke. When a cotter pin hinge has been replaced—usually by a later, stronger type—the scars left by the cotter pins are often clearly visible and serve as an excellent clue to age. This type of hinge was used from the earliest days of our country until early in the nineteenth century. Therefore, a country piece found either with authentic cotter pin hinges or with evidence of them can be dated with confidence prior to 1820. These hinges are found on the lids of chests and boxes exclusively, since they were almost completely unsuited to other applications.

155

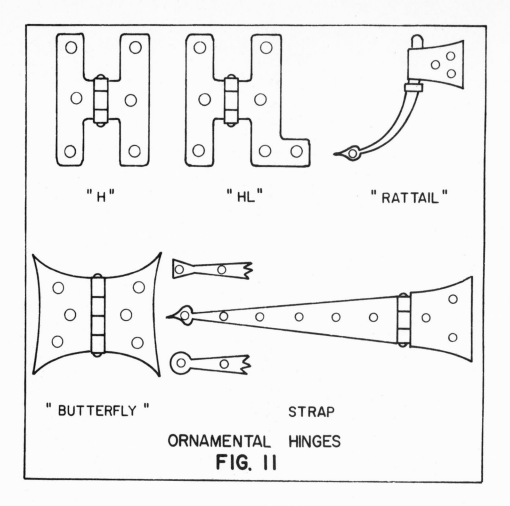

"H"　　　　　　"HL"　　　　　　"RATTAIL"

"BUTTERFLY"　　　　　　STRAP

ORNAMENTAL HINGES
FIG. 11

A type of hinge which is as old as the cotter pin hinge, but which did not remain popular as long, is the butterfly hinge (see Figure 11). This hinge predates the period we are studying, so we will give only a brief description to familiarize the reader with the type. It was an iron hinge—hand-forged, of course—and the forging resulted in a spreading at the corners, giving the hinge the appearance of a butterfly with spread wings. These hinges were used primarily on drop-leaf tables, but occasionally they were used on cupboard doors and desk box lids as well.

The most common "ornamental" hinges are the "H" and "HL" hinges. They were used only on cupboard doors, and a glance at Plate 103 or at Figure 11 will leave little doubt as to how they got their names. On country furniture, at least, they are usually of hand-forged iron and quite sturdily made. Even the strongest hinges are vulnerable, however, so a piece complete with its full com-

103. Hand-forged iron "H" hinge. Notice heads of the hand-forged nails.

Photograph by Charles R. Steitz, Jr.

plement of original "H" or "HL" hinges is hard to find. A country piece equipped with all of its original *brass* "H" or "HL" hinges is a rarity indeed, since brass, which is less hardy than iron, was seldom used on country furniture.

Ornamental hinges were usually attached by hand-forged nails, although screws were occasionally used. As mentioned earlier, the type of nail or screw can be an important clue to the age of the piece or to the authenticity of the hinge. If the hinges themselves are original, they also can be useful in estimating age, since 1820 is usually accepted as about the latest date when hand-forged hinges were used.

An early ornamental hinge that was almost exclusively of Pennsylvania provenance was the "rat-tail" hinge (see Plate 104 and Figure 11). This deceptively strong hinge was always hand-forged of iron and was used only on cupboards. Its period of use was roughly contemporary to that of "H" and "HL" hinges. The stationary part of the hinge was curved and tapered, just like a rat's tail, but the pointed end was flattened into a sort of arrowhead, which, as Nutting points out, makes it look more like a devil's tail than a rat's. This tail was mounted on the outside of the cupboard and fastened at two places: at the lower end (the arrowhead) by a hand-forged nail, and a short distance from the top of the tail by a staple. This staple was driven entirely through the wood and clinched, thus providing a stop for the movable part of the hinge as well as an anchor for the top end of the tail. Without the staple the movable part would be free to slide too far down the tail.

The movable part of the hinge was usually attached to the cupboard door by hand-forged nails. If it was a flush door, the hinge was mounted onto the outside, but if the door was lipped, the hinge was driven into the edge of the door just behind the lip, as in Plate 104. In the latter case hand-forged nails were driven through the face of the door and through the hinge. Cupboard doors mounted on rat-tail hinges can be removed simply by opening the door and lifting, thus separating the two parts of each hinge.

Now quite rare, cupboards equipped with rat-tail hinges command high prices, so a would-be purchaser would be wise to examine the hinges closely to be sure that they are all original.

Another hinge now considered decorative is the iron strap hinge found on early chests. Although these hinges seem ornamental to us today, they were meant to be strictly functional, and any decoration they may carry is the result of a blacksmith's desire to add a little something extra to his work. For this reason, strap hinges are found tapered almost to a point, with the tapered end then expanded into one of several different shapes, the most common of which are shown in Figure 11. The arrowhead strap hinge is also illustrated in Plate 105. They were usually used on the inside of chests and were attached by hand-

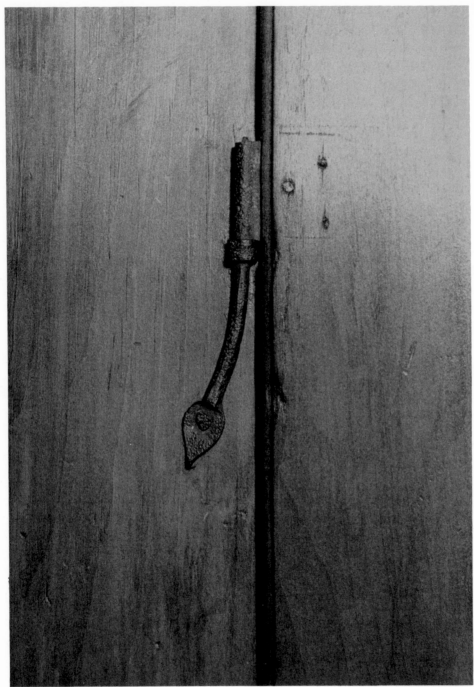

104. Hand-forged rat-tail hinge   *Photograph by Charles R. Steitz, Jr.*

105. Painted and dated blanket chest showing arrowhead strap hinges
Courtesy of The Mercer Museum, Doylestown, Pennsylvania   Photograph by Charles R. Steitz, Jr.

forged nails, or screws, or both. Quite frequently a chest is found with the hinge attached by five or six screws (or nails) through each leaf, supplemented by a large rivet driven completely through the wood and flattened against the hinge. A chest with this arrangement is often found with the original hinges still held securely by the rivets, while most of the screws (or nails) have worked loose and been lost.

Since our early cabinetmakers did not consider strap hinges to be decorative, they were faced with the problem of keeping them out of sight. This problem was not as simple as it might sound. Since it is a practical impossibility to

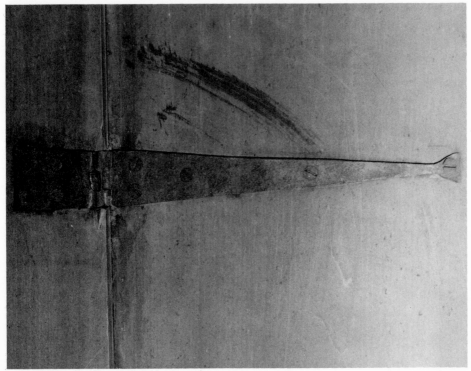

106. Offset strap hinge. Notice the large nail through the offset.

Photograph by Charles R. Steitz, Jr.

mount a straight strap hinge on the inside of a chest, the cabinetmaker was left with two alternatives: he could either fasten one leaf to the outside of the chest, or he could offset the hinge—that is, change the planes of the leaves by introducing a 90-degree angle into one of them. The latter method (see Figure 12 and Plate 106) seemed to be the more desirable, but it was found that the offset portion of the hinge tended to straighten out with use. This problem was solved by driving a large hand-forged nail through the offset into the edge of the back board of the chest; most chests found with offset hinges are also found with these nails. (Again see Figure 12 and Plate 106.)

A "non-decorative" hinge that was in use long before the period under consideration (and is still in use) is the common butt hinge. It was, and still is, used to mount cupboard doors in such a way that a minimum of metal (just the barrel of the hinge) is visible. The butt hinge was also used on woodboxes and later on chests, thus eliminating the necessity of using the offset strap hinge. The earliest butt hinges were made of two sheets of hand-forged iron, rolled over a pin that went through the entire length of the joint. In about 1830 the cheaper cast iron butt hinge became available and rapidly replaced hand-forged

161

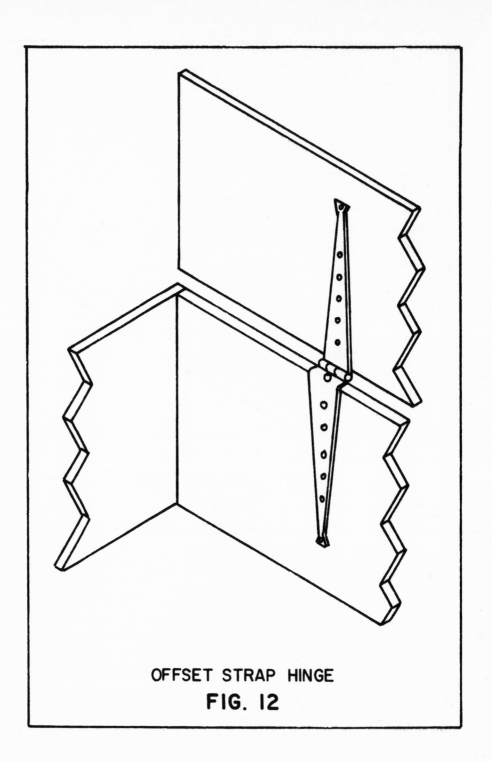

OFFSET STRAP HINGE

FIG. 12

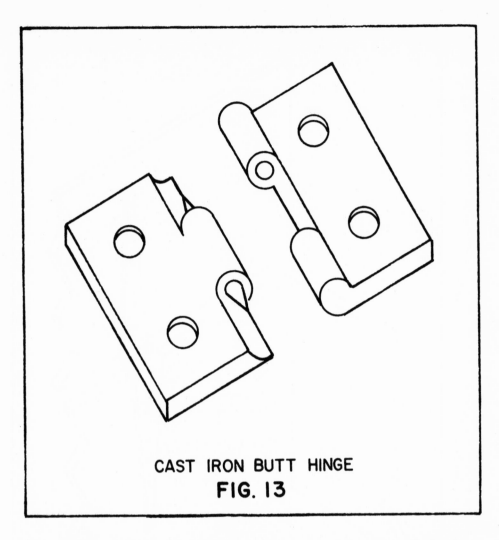

CAST IRON BUTT HINGE
FIG. 13

hinges on all but the finest of furniture. The cast iron butt hinge had only a rudimentary pin (see Figure 13) which, coupled with the brittle nature of cast iron, usually resulted in a rather short life and quick replacement.

In addition to being fragile, the cast iron hinge was heavy and bulky, so that when a lighter stamped butt hinge was developed early in the twentieth century, it replaced the cast iron hinge almost immediately. As with hand-forged hinges, the joint of the stamped butt hinge was rolled around the pin. This is the hinge that we buy in hardware stores today.

A different type of cast iron butt hinge was found on the wardrobe shown in Plate 44. This hinge (see Figure 14) combined the best features of the rat-

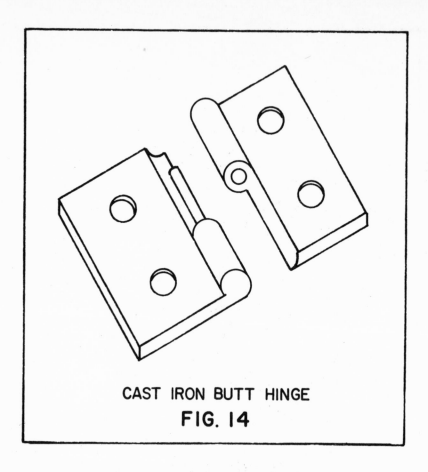

CAST IRON BUTT HINGE
FIG. 14

tail hinge and the butt hinge. Very little metal is visible, and the door can be removed from the piece simply by opening it and lifting straight up, just as if it were equipped with a set of rat-tail hinges.

Brass butt hinges were used extensively on more formal city furniture but seldom on country-made pieces.

Drawer Pulls

In the field of fine furniture, "drawer pulls" and "brasses" are practically synonymous, but in this study of country furniture, on which brass hardware was seldom used, we feel justified in dismissing the entire subject of brasses with little further ado. Brass hardware was not used on pre-Revolutionary furniture primarily because of its cost—brass foundries were prohibited by law in the Colonies, so any hardware of this type had to be imported from England at great expense. Even when brass hardware became available, the prudence of our country folk, along with their resistance to change, tended to exclude it. By the

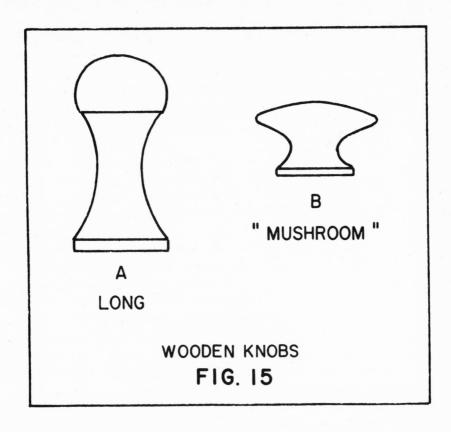

B

" MUSHROOM "

A

LONG

WOODEN KNOBS

FIG. 15

time they became style-conscious enough to accept it, the Empire style, with its revival of wooden knobs, was being felt even in rural areas. Thus, it can be seen that brass hardware played a very small part in the production of the furniture in which we are interested.

Although wooden knobs probably should not properly be classified as hardware, they were used in lieu of hardware on most of our country furniture, so it is in this light that we shall study them.

The earliest pieces of the period under discussion were equipped with knobs shaped like the one in Figure 15A. This particular one was sketched from a knob used as a combination pull and latch for a cupboard door, but similarly shaped ones were also used as drawer pulls on country pieces until the beginning of the nineteenth century. These early wooden knobs were quite long (up to 3 inches) compared to the squatty, mushroom-shaped later ones. While the mushroom knobs were considerably shorter than the early ones, projecting at the most only about an inch from the face of the piece, they were often much greater in diameter, sometimes measuring as much as 2½ inches across (see Figure 15B). These mushroom knobs became popular about 1820 and remained so, at least in rural Pennsylvania, until well into the twentieth century.

Early wooden knobs were fastened to the piece by the simple expedient of driving the shaft, which was an integral part of the knob, into a slightly undersized hole in the piece. This was not a very secure arrangement, and consequently, very few of these knobs are found today. Later ones were fastened by means of a threaded dowel which was screwed into both the knob and the piece. Still later ones were secured by a screw which was inserted from the back of the piece (a drawer front, for instance) into the base of the knob.

In 1825 the first patent was granted for pressed glass knobs, which subsequently became quite popular in city and country alike. These were attached to the piece by means of a threaded brass or iron post, imbedded in a plaster core in the center of the knob. This was not a particularly strong arrangement, and it is a rare piece that has all its original glass knobs intact. Excellent reproductions are available in many of the patterns of these old glass knobs, so it is sometimes possible to match the new with the old in order to complete a set. For the same reason, however, one should thoroughly investigate all the knobs on a piece said to be "all original" in order to determine whether this claim is, in fact, true. It is quite easy to differentiate between the new and the old in this case, since the old ones will have posts fitted with irregularly shaped nuts. The advent of machine-cut threads, which was almost contemporary with the invention of pressed glass knobs, practically eliminated the use of hand-threaded posts quite early in the history of these knobs, so we must rely on the irregularly shaped nuts, which were used until about 1860, in our differentiation of new from old. Nuts made after 1860 were invariably square or hexagonal.

The carved leaf and fruit pull of the Victorian era fortunately did not gain wide popularity in rural Pennsylvania until after the advent of machine-made furniture. Since this puts them beyond the period of our interest, we can dismiss the whole subject with a sigh of relief.

The white procelain knobs that we see in such quantities today did not come onto the scene until the closing years of the nineteenth century. They achieved immediate popularity, probably because of the ease with which they could be used to replace broken or lost wooden knobs and because of the touch of elegance they gave to otherwise rather plain furniture.

Keyhole Escutcheons

The keyholes on the earliest of our country pieces were completely innocent of ornamentation, but it was not long until the advantage of protective metal became apparent and the escutcheon came into use. The first escutcheons were of hand-forged iron, either oval, diamond-shaped, or rectangular with trimmed corners (see Figure 16). Although the material changed to brass,

KEYHOLE ESCUTCHEONS
FIG. 16

sheet iron, and even porcelain in later years, these basic shapes—with a few others, such as the shield and heart—remained in general use throughout the entire period we are considering.

An interesting innovation can be seen on the chest of drawers in Plate 27: The escutcheons are diamond shaped, but they are made of hardwood (maple) instead of metal and are inlaid into the drawer fronts.

Locks

Volumes have been written on locks and on the intricate and ingenious methods that locksmiths have devised to provide safe places for people to store their valuables. But since we are dealing with country furniture, we will confine our attention to the locks most commonly used by our country cabinetmakers, and at that, we will only be able to scratch the surface.

As in most other lock applications, furniture locks are usually mounted on the movable member of the piece. For example, cupboard locks are mounted on the doors, and drawer locks are mounted on the drawer fronts (on the inside in both cases, of course). The one notable exception to this rule is found on any piece of furniture with a hinged lid, such as a chest or a schoolmaster's desk.

The most common type of cabinet lock is that found on cupboard doors and drawer fronts. This type, for want of a better name, we shall call a box lock, since a small metal box is all that most of us ever see of the lock, even when it is removed from the piece. This lock is mounted on the inside of the door or drawer so that the bolt, when extended by a turn of the key, engages a slot in the frame of the piece. The slot can be faced by a metal plate, but more often than not on country furniture it is merely a narrow mortice in the wood. The key is inserted by way of a keyhole cut through the front of the

167

piece and matching the keyhole in the lock itself. Locks of this type made before 1800 usually had rather thick bolts; these gradually gave way to broader and thinner bolts, until by the end of the nineteenth century they had become the blade-like tongues that we see on modern furniture. This type of lock can be unlocked *and* locked only by using the key.

On chests and some desks we find a different type of lock, one that is mounted on the stationary front of the piece rather than on the movable member. In this arrangement, a tongue, mounted on the inside of the lid of the piece, drops into the lock, and is caught and held by one device or another. The earliest of these locks have a hand-forged tongue (or "keeper"), shaped like an arrowhead, which usually is fastened to the inside of the lid by a large hand-forged rivet. When the lid is closed, this keeper drops between two iron "claws" held together by a fairly heavy spring; thus, the chest is locked simply by closing the lid, and the key is used only to open the chest. The oldest of these locks had exposed claws, much like the claws of a crab, so they became known as crab locks. Later locks, while operating on the same principle, were completely enclosed in a metal case, so that the keeper had to drop through a slot in the case in order to reach the claws.

On most desks and later chests, the arrowhead-shaped keeper was replaced by a projecting tongue with a lateral hole through it, which was screwed to the bottom of the lid. This type of keeper was engaged by a bolt within the lock when the key was turned to lock the piece, and it was disengaged when the key was turned in the opposite direction.

The locks we have just discussed were usually made of iron, hand-forged in the earlier ones and machine-made later. Some delicate brass locks are found on bride's boxes, desks, and chests of drawers. The exception again is the crab lock, which was always made of iron.

Locks in general were expensive, so our early cabinetmakers often went to great lengths to minimize their use. They accomplished this by many ingenious devices which enabled the various sections of a piece to be secured from within the one section equipped with a lock. Thus, the drawers beneath a slant-top desk might be secured from within the desk proper, or all the drawers of a chest of drawers might be secured from a position behind the top drawer, which had the only metal lock on the piece.

Catches

Although iron and brass catches were used to some extent on early country furniture, particularly on cupboards, wooden catches by far outnumbered the metal. While the simple turn button was used extensively, the more elaborate arrangement shown in Plate 107 seems to have been more popular. The

168

107. Wooden catch on a Montgomery County jelly cupboard

Photograph by Charles R. Steitz, Jr.

latter type of catch, which was mounted on (and through) the cupboard door, was preferred over a turn button because in addition to securing the door, it simultaneously provided a knob to open and close it. The knob and shaft were turned from a single piece of hardwood, and the catch, merely a blade of wood, was inserted through a slot in the shaft in such a way that rotating the knob would position the catch behind the door frame, thus fastening the door. This type of catch was used on country cupboards through the first quarter of the nineteenth century.

Brass and iron catches, essentially similar to the wooden ones just discussed, were used over approximately the same span of years as the wooden ones. They were equipped with a flat blade which slipped onto a square threaded shaft and was held in place by a nut. On the earliest catches, of course, the threads on the shaft were hand-cut, and the nut was irregularly shaped.

Pieces equipped with locks frequently had no catch at all, the lock bolt being relied upon to keep the door closed. These could be opened only by turning the key, which was sometimes required to do double duty as a knob.

Hand-forged catches of wrought iron are occasionally encountered and are highly prized. They were the results of the ingenuity of individual blacksmiths, and consequently, no two are alike. The presence of such a catch on a country cupboard greatly increases the value of the piece.

Spring-loaded slide catches were a factory-made product of the Victorian era. The presence of this type of catch on a cupboard or dry sink indicates a late, not particularly desirable specimen—provided, of course, that the catch was originally part of the piece, and not a later addition.

CHAPTER ELEVEN

MODIFICATIONS AND ALTERATIONS

Authenticity and originality are the keynotes of the entire range of antique collecting, and this is particularly true with regard to furniture. A piece that is "all original" is always considerably more desirable and valuable than a piece that has been modified or altered in any way, regardless of the reason for alteration. It is not uncommon today to find pieces that have had something done to them over the years to change them in one manner or another from their original form. More often than not, these changes were made by subsequent owners to fit their own particular needs and/or tastes.

Fortunately for our peace of mind, the fraudulent production of country antiques has never become particularly widespread, since the cost of creating a bogus piece is just too high for the practice to be economically attractive. This situation will continue to exist as long as country antiques remain available at modest prices, and no longer. As soon as a faker feels he can sell a fraudulent piece for more than it would cost to produce it, the race will be on.

In this chapter we will point out some of the more common modifications and alterations found in country furniture and attempt to show how they may be recognized.

Marriage

Probably the most common alteration seen in country furniture is the joining, or "marriage" of the top section of a cupboard to an entirely unrelated bottom section. This is a simple operation, requiring a minimum of labor. All that is really needed is a bottom section slightly larger than the top and an eye for matching stain. Often the only new wood added is for the molding used to keep the top section properly positioned on the bottom.

A marriage is usually as simple to detect as it is to accomplish. The first place to examine is the back of the cupboard, since it would be a rare marriage indeed in which the back boards of the top and bottom sections match. There is usually an immediately discernible difference in the color, texture, or size of the corresponding boards used in the backs of the two sections if they were not made at the same time and place and by the same craftsman.

The ends of the molding that hold the top section in place should also be examined. Raw, freshly cut end grain on this molding indicates that it has recently been replaced, possibly in the course of normal restoration but also possibly as part of an attempt to deceive.

The top and bottom sections of an authentic piece will always be of similar, if not identical, construction. If wooden pegs are found in the stile and rail joints of one section and not the other, or if the sides are nailed to the back in one section and the reverse is true in the other, the piece should be viewed with serious doubt.

Alteration

It often became desirable to change the basic style of a piece of furniture to conform to a style currently in vogue. In the parlance of the trade, a piece that has been so treated is a "monkey." We will discuss briefly some of the monkeys occasionally encountered.

Dutch cupboards converted into Welsh dressers

This was accomplished by removing the doors from the top section of a Dutch cupboard and scrolling the edges of the door frames. It can usually be detected by the presence of modern tool marks in the scrolling and by nail holes or plugs indicating that a vertical portion of frame has been removed from the center of the top section.

Drawers added to tables

When an old drawer has been added to an old table, the best clue to the alteration is again found in the end grain of the old wood. A rectangle must be cut out of the apron of the table to insert the drawer, and the end grain on either side of that rectangle will be lighter than the other surfaces. If an old drawer was substituted for a missing original one, the chances are a thousand to one that the replacement had to be altered in one way or another to make it fit. It would have to have been built up, cut down, lengthened or shortened, and in any case the alteration should be quite obvious.

Feet added to chests

Chests designed to rest flat on the floor are often found with feet that were added later, no doubt with an eye to increasing the desirability of the piece. The feet are usually either simple bracket feet or turned feet, and when well done, they do indeed improve the appearance of the piece. Although added feet can be made to look quite convincing at first glance, the deception becomes apparent when the bottom of the chest is examined. Any chest that has rested flat on the floor for one hundred years or more will have acquired a bottom surface covered with scratches and gouges. Conversely, a chest originally built with feet will have a bottom surface that although darkened by age to a pleasing patina, will be relatively free of marks.

Solid panels replaced by glass

Occasionally a cupboard is found in which the original solid panels of the top doors have been replaced by glass panes. This type of modification can usually be spotted by the workmanship of the alteration. The mullions holding the glass panes usually do not match the molding of the frame, and the horizontal mullions probably do not line up with the edges of the shelves behind them. We have seen a piece in which the modifier did not even bother to mortice the mullions into the frame, as was always done on authentic pieces.

Thinned-out bed posts

Unfortunately, at one time high-post beds with slender posts became more fashionable than those with chubby posts. This was an easy alteration to accomplish and a hard one to detect. It was done by putting the posts in a lathe and simply removing some of the wood. About the only way to spot this kind of modification is by comparing the square sections of the posts, where the rails are fastened, to the turned sections. If there seems to be too much wood in the square sections, the bed is suspect. The patina on the posts can also be compared to that on the rest of the bed, but the chances are that time has already taken care of that detail.

Hardware

As we have said before, hardware of every kind is easy to replace, but fortunately, the replacement is usually just as easy to detect. Almost invariably, we can find marks, such as dents and plugged holes, which have been left on the wood by the old hardware and which are quite obvious under close examination.

If reproduction hardware is used instead of old, it usually gives itself away. Threads are noticeably machine-cut and nuts factory-made, and the marks found on old hardware, such as those left by the file on bevelled edges and the rough surfaces left by the sand mold on cast pieces, are conspicuously absent. Holes on the reproduction hardware might be uniformly off center in each piece of a set, and the surface might have the rough "hammered" look that so many people consider "authentic Early American."

Restoration

There are many restorations that are not only perfectly acceptable but often vitally necessary to the rehabilitation of antiques into usable pieces of furniture. Restoration is undesirable only when it is extensive enough to reduce the value of a piece and when the piece is offered for sale with no mention of the restoration. Restorations such as new feet on a table or chair, a new leg, rung, or spindle on a chair, or a new top on a table all reduce the value of the piece to varying degrees, but they are quite acceptable as long as they are pointed out by the seller. Normally, such restorations are quite easily detected when the furniture is left in the rough or finished in natural wood, but when a piece such as a chair is repainted and redecorated, the restorations can be quite difficult to find without close examination.

In trying to point out a few of the pitfalls that can trap a novice venturing into the field of country furniture, we sincerely hope that we have not discouraged anyone from continuing to study and acquire country antiques. Only by ownership can one feel the deep sense of satisfaction that comes from living with and *using* the articles produced by our early country craftsmen. Much of this satisfaction comes from knowing that the furniture was built by men who wanted it to last and who used methods calculated to make it last. Fortunately, "planned obsolescence" is a catch phrase invented by men of the twentieth century and had no place in the vocabulary of our forefathers.

We have attempted throughout this book to begin to answer the question that is heard so often, "How do you *know* that it is old?" But we would like to emphasize that this is only a beginning. For the novice just becoming interested in antiques, there are literally hundreds of volumes to read, but (and we quote a wise man) "reading is only part of understanding antiques." By this he meant that a real "feel" for good antiques is developed by a combination of reading, seeing, and touching. For the "seeing," we suggest visits to some of the many excellent museums throughout the country. For the "touching," nothing beats a good country auction, unless it is the shop of an understanding dealer.

SIGNS

	SAW MARKS			BIT HOLES			DOVETAILS		
	PIT SAW	GASH SAW	CIRCULAR SAW	POD	GIMLET POINT	SCORE MARKS	COLONIAL	VICTORIAN	MACHINE
1750									
1775									
1800									
1825									
1850									
1875									
1900									

PINS	NAILS		SCREWS			COTTER PIN	BUTTER FLY	HINGES			
	FORGED	CUT	FORGED	MACHINE	GIMLET			DECORATIVE	STRAP	FORGED BUTT	CAST BUTT

GLOSSARY

Below are listed some of the words and phrases that have been used in the preceding chapters and that are peculiar to the jargon of antique collectors and dealers. We list them in the hope that they may be of some assistance to those of our readers who are just beginning to develop a serious interest in the arts and artifacts of our forebears.

Apron   That part of a table immediately below the top, which is fastened to the top and which joins and supports the legs.

Auger   A device for drilling holes in wood. A bit.

Bail   The handle of some drawer pulls. It is shaped like the bail, or handle, of a bucket.

Bamboo turning   A turning which resembles the shape of a bamboo stalk.

Batten   A piece of wood used to hold other pieces of wood together. Often found on the undersides of tabletops and chest lids. Also used to strengthen and/or prevent warping. Also called a cleat.

Beaded   The term applied to the small half-round molding sometimes found on doors and more often on drawers.

Bracket feet   A type of feet found on case pieces and chests. They can be (or can appear to be) extensions of the front, back, and sides. Usually scrolled or angled from the floor to the bottom of the piece.

Bureau desk   A case piece, usually composed of a series of drawers surmounted by a desk with a slant front. The slant front is hinged at the bottom and is lowered to provide a writing surface.

Burl   The large knob, or protuberance, found on the side of some hardwood trees. Used to make beautifully grained and durable wooden bowls.

Butt joint   A method of joining two pieces of wood in which one is simply fastened to the end (or edge) of the other. Also the name given to the drop-leaf joint in which the square edge of the leaf meets the square edge of the top.

Cane seat   A chair seat woven of cane, usually in a geometric pattern of eight-sided or more holes.

Case piece   Any piece of furniture composed of a frame and an outside casing, such as a desk, a chest of drawers, or a cupboard.

Chest   To quote Nutting: "Strictly a receptacle with a lid, and generally a small till at one end. It may have no drawers, or one, two, and rarely three drawers."

Chest of drawers   A case piece composed of two or more drawers, with a flat top.

Cleat   See Batten.

Clinch   To bend over, as a nail is clinched after having been driven through a piece of wood.

Commode   A case piece designed to hold a pitcher and bowl. Usually has a towel bar above the top and one wide drawer just below the top, with a cupboard and sometimes two narrow drawers below the drawer.

Cotter pin hinge   An early hinge, found exclusively on chests and boxes, consisting of two cotter pins looped together and thrust diagonally through both members of the joint. Also called a staple hinge.

Crest rail   The top slat of a chair.

Dovetail   A method of joining two pieces of wood at a corner by a series of interlocking wedge-shaped tenons.

Drawer slide   That part of a piece upon which the side of a drawer runs.

Dresser   A type of cupboard composed of a top section with open shelves and an enclosed bottom section.

Drop-leaf   Refers to a specific type of table with leaves that fold down when not in use. See Leaf.

Empire   That style of furniture that was produced in America from 1820 to 1840 (about 1830 to 1850 in the rural areas).

Escutcheon   A metal, porcelain, or wooden ornament mounted on the front of a keyhole.

Field bed   A bed much like a tester bed, except that the frame from which the canopy was hung was arched, so that in outline the bed resembled a tent.

Finial   The decorative top end of a post (chair post, bedpost, etc.).

Flush   Refers to surfaces that are in the same plane. For example, flush drawers are those that are made so that when closed their fronts are in the same plane as the surrounding front surface of the piece.

Fly bracket   The swinging arm used to support the leaf of a drop-leaf table.

Gate leg   The movable leg of a table that swings out from the apron to support a drop leaf. Also the name of a specific type of table.

Gimlet   The screw point on the end of a modern wood bit.

Graining   A decoration which simulates the natural grain of wood.

Groove joint   The name given to a drop-leaf joint in which the top is grooved to receive a tongue formed on the edge of the leaf, or vice-versa.

Hand-forged   Refers to metal articles, principally iron, which were handmade, usually by a blacksmith. Forging was accomplished by heating the metal and hammering it into the desired shape.

Hutch   A small box or cubby. Used to describe a chair-table with a top that can be raised or lowered and with a storage bin beneath the seat. Incorrectly used to describe an open-top cupboard (Welsh dresser).

Jack plane   A large smoothing plane.

Kas   A large wardrobe-like case piece of Dutch origin.

Keeler   A wooden maple sugar bucket.

Keeper   That part of a lock which is engaged by the bolt (or some other device) and which prevents the piece from being opened when locked.

Ladder-back   Refers to a chair with a back composed of several narrow slats.

Leaf   The movable part of a tabletop, usually hinged so that it hangs straight down when not in use.

Lipped   Refers to cupboard door fronts or drawer fronts that have a small molding around the edge, which prevents the drawer or the door from going all the way into the piece.

Livery cupboard   An English case piece, partially enclosed by spindles. Used for the storage of food.

Marriage   A cupboard composed of two dissimilar sections.

Molding   A decorative strip of wood often applied to case pieces.

Mortice   A slot cut into one member of a joint to receive a tenon on the other member.

Mortice and tenon joint   A joint in which one piece is cut out (morticed) to receive a projection (tenon) on the other.

Mullions   The horizontal and vertical strips of wood into which glass panes are set.

Offset hinge   A strap hinge most often found on chests. One leaf of the hinge has a 90-degree bend, which allows both leaves to be located on the inside of the chest.

Panel   A board which fills the space within the frame in stile and rail construction. Usually set into a groove in the edge of the stile or rail.

Patina   The complexion or hue that is imparted to wood by time and exposure to air.

Pawl   As used in this book, a pivoted tongue on the stationary frame of a candle stand which engages notches on a movable vertical rod. The rod (which holds the candles) can be raised at will, but the pawl must be disengaged from the notches before the rod can be lowered.

Pembroke   Name given to a particular style of drop-leaf table.

Picker   One who travels the countryside, buying antiques privately and at auction for resale to dealers.

Pie crust   The raised rim found on some exceptionally good tables and stands.

Pigeon hole   Small cubby within a desk.

Pin   A hard wooden peg, whittled into a point and driven into a hole bored in a joint. Used to secure a joint much as a nail would. Also called a trenail.

Pod bit   An early auger, used for drilling holes in wood.

Post   A vertical member of a chair back. Also a vertical member of a bed frame.

Provenance   Origin or source.

Pulls   Hardware attached to drawer fronts, used to pull the drawers open.

Rake   The angle or "splay" of table or chair legs.

Ring turning   Style of turning (on a lathe) that resembles a series of rings.

Rung   See Stretcher.

Rule joint   Name given to the drop-leaf joint in which the edge of the top and the edge of the leaf are shaped like the joint of a carpenter's rule.

Rush seat   A chair seat woven of rushes or reeds.

Sawbuck   Table trestle shaped like an "X". Also the name of a specific type of table.

Scalloped   Cut in a series of arcs, much like the edge of a scallop shell.

Score marks   Marks used on chair legs and posts to locate the positions of slats and rungs.

Scribe   A carpenter's marking tool. Used to scratch construction marks on wood.

Slat   A horizontal back member of a chair.

Socket   The hole which receives any turned member.

182

Spindle   A turned vertical member of a chair.

Splat   The wide, central, upright member of a chair back.

Splint seat   A chair seat woven of split hickory splints.

Spool turning   Style of turning (on a lathe) that resembles a series of thread spools.

Stile and rail   A type of frame construction in which the horizontal members (rails) are morticed into the vertical members (stiles) and a panel is set in between the members.

Strap hinge   A hinge most often found on chests and today considered to be decorative. It consists of two straps each from 7 to 15 inches long, and up to 2 inches wide at the pin, the longer end tapering almost to a point and then swelling to a decorative finial.

Stretcher   That member of a table or chair that connects the legs. Used for bracing. When turned, a chair stretcher is called a rung.

Survival piece   A piece of furniture in which style or construction features recall a period prior to its date of manufacture.

Tavern table (large)   A table with stretchers connecting the legs near the bottom. Usually with one or more drawers in the apron.

Tavern table (small)   A small, light table used in early taverns for serving individuals who did not wish to sit at the common table.

Tenon   A projection on one member of a joint, designed to fit into a mortice in the other member.

Tester Bed   A high-post bed with a plain, flat frame from which a canopy (or tester) was hung.

Till   A small box with a hinged lid usually found at one end of a chest.

Toe-nailed   Joined by nailing at an angle from a face of one piece into the face of another. A method frequently seen on tables, where the top is secured by nails driven through the inside face of the apron into the bottom side of the top.

Treenware   Utensils made of wood.

Trenail   See Pin.

Trestle   A braced frame, or "horse," used to support a table top. Also the name of a specific type of table.

Tripod   Any piece of furniture with three legs. Usually refers to tables.

Turn button   Usually just a small piece of wood, mounted on the frame of a cupboard in such a way that when turned to a horizontal position, it prevents the door from opening.

Turned   Shaped on a lathe, as a table or chair leg.

Vase turning   Style of turning (on a lathe) that resembles the shape of a vase.

Victorian   The name of a period of furniture style covering the last half of the nineteenth century.

Wash stand   A piece of furniture designed to hold a pitcher and bowl. Usually contains a low shelf and a drawer but is never enclosed beneath the drawer.

Wrought iron   The iron used in forging utensils and hardware such as hinges and catches.

BIBLIOGRAPHY

Andrews, Edward Deming and Faith. *Shaker Furniture*. New York: Dover Publications, Inc., 1950.

Brazer, Ester Stephens. *Early American Decoration*. Springfield, Mass.: Pond-Ekberg Company, 1947.

Comstock, Helen (Ed.). *The Concise Encyclopedia of American Antiques*. New York: Hawthorne Books, Inc., 1965.

Drepperd, Carl W. *A Dictionary of American Antiques*. Boston: Charles T. Branford Company, 1952.

Gloag, John and Bridgewater, Derek. *A History of Cast Iron Architecture*. London: George Allen and Unwin Ltd., 1948.

Grotz, George. *The Furniture Doctor*. Garden City, New York: Doubleday & Company, Inc., 1962.

——— *From Gunk to Glow*. Deep River, Conn.: New Era Press, Inc., 1952.

Hayden, Arthur. *Chats on Cottage and Farmhouse Furniture*. New York: A. A. Wyn, Inc., 1950.

Kettell, Russell Hawes. *The Pine Furniture of Early New England*. Garden City, New York: Doubleday, Doran and Company, Inc., 1929.

Lipman, Jean and Meulendyke, Eve. *American Folk Decoration*. New York: Oxford University Press, Inc., 1951.

Lockwood, Luke Vincent. *Colonial Furniture in America*. New York: Charles Scribner's Sons, 1926. 2 vols.

Marsh, Moreton. *The Easy Expert in Collecting and Restoring American Antiques*. Philadelphia, Pa.: J. B. Lippincott Company, 1959.

McKearin, Helen and George S. *Two Hundred Years of American Blown Glass*. New York: Crown Publishers, Inc., 1949, 1950.

185

Nutting, Wallace. *Furniture Treasury*. New York: The Macmillan Company, 1928. 3 vols.

Ormsbee, Thomas Hamilton. *Field Guide to Early American Furniture*. Boston: Little, Brown and Company, 1960.

———— *The Windsor Chair*. New York: Hearthside Press, 1962.

Robacker, Earl F. *Pennsylvania Dutch Stuff: A Guide to Country Antiques*. Philadelphia, Pa.: University of Pennsylvania Press, 1944.

Shiffer, Margaret Berwind. *Furniture and Its Makers of Chester County, Pennsylvania*. Philadelphia, Pa.: University of Pennsylvania Press, 1966.

Taylor, Henry Hammond. *Knowing, Collecting and Restoring Early American Furniture*. Philadelphia, Pa.: J. B. Lippincott Company, 1930.

Williams, H. Lionel. *Country Furniture of Early America*. New York: A. S. Barnes, 1963.

INDEX

Fairfield, the text type of this book, is both slightly decorative and extremely legible. It was designed for Linotype by Rudolph Ruzicka and is one of the most handsome and useful of twentieth-century typefaces.